OTHER INDONESIANS

OXFORD STUDIES IN THE ANTHROPOLOGY OF LANGUAGE

Series editor: Alessandro Duranti, *University of California at Los Angeles*

This series is devoted to works from a wide array of scholarly traditions that treat linguistic practices as forms of social action.

Thank You for Dying for Our Country: Commemorative Texts and Performances in Jerusalem
Chaim Noy

Singular and Plural: Ideologies of Linguistic Authority in 21st Century Catalonia
Kathryn A. Woolard

Linguistic Rivalries: Tamil Migrants and Anglo-Franco Conflicts
Sonia Neela Das

The Monologic Imagination
Edited by Matt Tomlinson and Julian Millie

Looking like a Language, Sounding like a Race: Raciolinguistic Ideologies and the Learning of Latinidad
Jonathan Rosa

Talking like Children: Language and the Production of Age in the Marshall Islands
Elise Berman

The Struggle for a Multilingual Future: Youth and Education in Sri Lanka
Christina P. Davis

The Last Language on Earth: Linguistic Utopianism in the Philippines
Piers Kelly

Rethinking Politeness with Henri Bergson
Edited by Alessandro Duranti

OTHER INDONESIANS

Nationalism in an Unnative Language

Joseph Errington

OXFORD
UNIVERSITY PRESS

OXFORD
UNIVERSITY PRESS

Oxford University Press is a department of the University of Oxford. It furthers
the University's objective of excellence in research, scholarship, and education
by publishing worldwide. Oxford is a registered trade mark of Oxford University
Press in the UK and certain other countries.

Published in the United States of America by Oxford University Press
198 Madison Avenue, New York, NY 10016, United States of America.

CIP data is on file at the Library of Congress

ISBN 978–0–19–756368–7 (pbk.)
ISBN 978–0–19–756367–0 (hbk.)

DOI: 10.1093/oso/9780197563670.001.0001

9 8 7 6 5 4 3 2 1

Paperback printed by Marquis, Canada
Hardback printed by Bridgeport National Bindery, Inc., United States of America

In memory of
Bernard Bate
Harold Conklin
Jennifer Jackson
Michael Silverstein

CONTENTS

FOREWORD

I came to Indonesian in the mid-1970s as a "gateway" to Javanese, a language which attracted me as part of Java's celebrated tradition of performance arts. It seemed by comparison a simple language distinguished more by what it lacked than what it possessed. Only after some time living in different parts of Indonesia did I begin to recognize and take seriously the linguistic and social complexities of this language, and start considering gaps between norms of the standard language and the ways Indonesians speak.

I draw here on major developments in linguistic anthropology to frame some specifics in relation to broader questions about Indonesian in social practice, and to draw out what Goenawan Mohamad calls the valuable paradox that is within it. Though written in English, I hope this book resonates in some ways with Indonesian readers' ideas and intuitions. I also ask their forgiveness for flaws and shortcomings which I have surely failed to correct: mohon dengan hormat supaya kesalahan dan kekurangannya dimaafkan.

ACKNOWLEDGMENTS

This book draws on research done between 2008 and 2011 under the auspices of a multi-person project, "In Search of Middle Indonesia," sponsored by the Royal Institute of Linguistics and Anthropology (KITLV) of the Netherlands. My first and deepest debt of gratitude is to the program heads, Gerry Van Klinken and Henk Schulte Nordholt, for their help as institutional supporters and deeply knowledgeable colleagues. I benefited also from meetings with other participants in that project over the course of the program, particularly Sylvia Tidey and Wenty Marina Minza, whose own research in the towns of Kupang and Pontianak became directly relevant for my own work. I am grateful to the KITLV also for enabling me to spend time in Leiden with Jermy Balukh, a colleague from Kupang, which helped enormously to frame selected parts of the large amount of material we assembled. During that summer my acquaintance with another project participant, Prof. Dr. Cornelis Lay *almarhum*, greatly helped to put some of that material in a broader political context.

During the research period I was only able to make two or three visits each year to three towns which were quite distant from each other. The regular work of the project was carried out by colleagues living in Kupang, Pontianak, and Ternate. The results of their sustained, painstaking work were coordinated and assembled, in turn, at the Linguistic Data Consortium (LDC) of the Max Planck Institute (MPI) for Evolutionary Anthropology, based in Jakarta.

The Jakarta director of the KITLV, Roger Tol, provided continual, crucial oversight of administrative matters. David Gil, professor at the MPI and head of the LDC, provided enormously helpful institutional support and the benefit of his deep knowledge of Indonesian linguistics. I am grateful also to Prof. Dr. Bambang Kaswanti Purwa, head of the Center for Linguistic and Cultural Research (*Pusat Kajian Bahasa dan Budaya*) at Atma Jaya, for sponsoring both the LDC and this project. Uri Tadmor, director of the LDC, was a constant source of technical support, intellectual contributions, and personal advice. Over two and a half years, beginning with a training session for participants, Uri was always generous with collegial expertise, companionship, and provided the template for questionnaires which were used in this research. On his departure from the LDC he put me in touch with his equally kind and helpful colleague Pak Slamet Urip, to whom I am likewise grateful. I wish before the project's end I had been able to spend more time in Jakarta with John Bowden, his successor at the LDC.

At the LDC, Dr. Bathseba Litamahuputty communicated on a regular basis with researchers and compiled material they produced with great professionalism. I am deeply grateful for her administrative ability, and her patience with a newcomer to large digital databases. She was generous also with her extensive knowledge of Malay dialects, particularly that spoken in Ternate. I learned something new every time we talked, and regret not being able to discuss that variety of Malay in this book. Terima kasih Bu Betty.

Regular communication and transfer of research results between these three towns, the LDC office in Jakarta, and me in the United States, was possible thanks to the digital infrastructure put in place by Bradley Taylor (using Filemaker Pro 9 and later ELAN 4.6 to transcribe and code recordings, and FileMaker Pro 10 to code interviews). Though I met Brad in Jakarta only once, I relied constantly on his expertise and oversight for gathering and transmitting research materials. Vittoria Heru, working in Jakarta, offered patient, prompt replies to sometimes clueless queries from Connecticut. Tom Conners was a valuable sounding board and companion who helped me ease into life in Jakarta after a long hiatus.

To write a concise and focused account, I have deferred discussion of our research in Ternate, capital of the Province of North Maluku, although that research helped me frame material from the other towns. I extend my thanks to those there who contributed: Djaenal Syahdan, Nurhaya Hajidin, Nurizah U. Yasin, and Mamat Jalil.

Research in the town of Kupang succeeded beyond my hopes thanks to two coordinators: Prof. Dr. John Haan of Universitas Cendana, and Dr. Jermy Balukh of the Institute for Foreign Languages (*Sekolah Tinggi Bahasa Asing*). They were generous with their time, advice, and insights, and oversaw long-term work by a team of cordial, conscientious researchers: makasi kepada Bobby Tassy, Bu Elsy, Erni Farida Sri Ulina Ginting, Geesty Dewi Korance Tamonob, Hilda Naley, Intan Wijayanti, Karolina Yunita Liwulangi, Maria Melda Selviana Madhi, Mirsa Umiyati, Nimrod Sombu, Polce Aryanto Bessie, Oktelda E. Kolioe, and Salmun Tasik. I owe special thanks also to Judy Jacob, Barbara Grimes, and Charles Grimes for making time to talk with me during my first visit to Kupang, and doing much to orient me to the complex situation I was just beginning to study.

Uri Tadmor, besides helping in Jakarta, helped enlist researchers similarly able and willing to undertake research into the town of Pontianak. I draw very selectively here from the hours of recordings they made, high-quality transcriptions they produced, and interviews they conducted. Our conversations during my visits in Pontianak were likewise important for pointing me in directions I would likely not otherwise have taken. Hence my deep thanks to Dian Beistita, Dr. Nurfitri Nugrahaningsih of the Department of International Relations at Tanjung Pura University, Bapak Suhardi, Bapak Suhendra, and Bapak Wahyudi Tarmiji Su'ib.

During the overlong time I have taken to write this book I have benefited from queries and feedback after some 20 presentations about material it contains. I am grateful in particular for comments by Asif Agha, Andrew Carruthers, Jamie Davidson, Mark Donahue, Dwi Novi Djenar, David Gil, Zane Goebel, Ariel Heryanto, Nicholas Himmelman, Joel Kuipers, Alan Rumsey, and Kristian Tamtamo.

Thanks to Sandro, Don, and anonymous reviewers for their patience and suggestions. My gratitude also to Zabou for kind permission to reproduce the photograph of her 2018 art project in Kupang on the cover.

However important the contributions of all these friends and colleagues have been, none are responsible for the ways I have used them here.

A NOTE ON TRANSCRIPTIONS

Most Indonesian and Malay forms are written in the standard spelling system of Indonesian established by the Ministry of National Education in 2009 (*Ejaan Bahasa Indonesia yang Disempurnakan*). I often use accents, as that system allows, to differentiate three types of speech sounds which are otherwise transcribed with a single character. The character /é/ represents a sound similar to the first part of the diphthong vowel in the standard American English pronunciation of 'say.' The character /è/ represents a sound more like the vowel in the word 'set.' The character /e/, with no accent, represents the speech sound called schwa, and is pronounced like the second vowel of the word 'data.' As appropriate I write schwa instead with the symbol from the International Phonetic Alphabet: ə.

I sometimes diverge from standard spelling to transcribe glottal stops, heard in the middle of the English interjection "uh-oh," with /q/, reserving the character /k/ to represent voiceless velar stops. Exceptions are found in standard spellings of names, for instance, the city Pontianak and the ethnonym "Dayak." The voiced velar fricative which distinguishes some varieties of Malay is transcribed with the character ɣ from the International Phonetic Alphabet.

Spelling conventions used by Indonesian authors, which vary across eras, are reproduced in quotations from their work.

LIST OF TABLES

LIST OF EXAMPLE GROUPS

LIST OF TRANSCRIPTS

LIST OF APPENDICES

1

A VALUABLE PARADOX

From the day they were named into public existence, Indonesia and its language have continually enabled and transformed each other. Before its baptism by anticolonial activists in 1928, Indonesian had been an instrument of rule for the Netherlands East Indies; by 1944 it was a language of revolution; a year later it was used to declare Indonesia's independence. In 1966 it became instrumental for a program of "accelerated modernization" that was prosecuted across a vast territory by an authoritarian, self-named New Order regime. Over the next 30 years millions of native speakers of hundreds of ethnic languages acquired it, and among members of the generation that came of age since the New Order's fall in 1998 Indonesian is the universally accepted language of the world's third-largest democracy.[1]

In 1978, the sociologist Joshua Fishman celebrated early phases of this top-down project of language development (*pembangunan bahasa*) as a linguistic "miracle." He applied this label to a state-driven program designed to propagate knowledge of language without "natural," pre-national connections to a native speaking group or territory. Fishman, like those overseeing that project, regarded this absence of native speakers as a condition that could enhance Indonesian's role as a vector of modernity in a broader integrative project being prosecuted on hundreds of far-flung islands.[2]

Crucially enabling this "miracle," in turn, was what Amy Liu has called the "language regime" of standard Indonesian (2015: 4). This regime was established by the state, acting as what she calls a "third party," to establish standard Indonesian's forms—"good and true" (*baik dan benar*)—and "delineate[. . .] which languages can be used when and where" (2015: 19). Indonesian for this reason could figure in political and economic change while avoiding linguistic marks of difference among a citizenry comprising more than 600 ethnic groups (2015: 5). In the context of the Cold War, the regime of the standard made Indonesian a striking solution to what were regarded in the West as widespread "language problems of developing nations" (Fishman

Other Indonesians. Joseph Errington, Oxford University Press. © Oxford University Press 2022.
DOI: 10.1093/oso/9780197563670.003.0001

et al. 1968). When members of a heteroglot citizenry acquired Indonsian as an instrument and symbol of modernity, it helped the New Order to "capture and monopolize" (Appadurai 1990: 303) a vision of national modernity.

In 1998 the New Order suddenly fell with the resignation of its leader, President Suharto. The ensuing period was marked by political instability, social unrest, and sporadic collective violence. Demands for autonomy from peripheral regions ushered in an era of *réformasi*—"one of the most radical decentralization programs attempted anywhere in the world" (Aspinall and Fealy 2003: 9)—as power devolved from Jakarta, apex and center of New Order power, to regional politicians and decision-makers.

The new political dispensation emerging from this disarray furnished grounds for some to argue against the "general, long-standing conclusion" that Indonesia's unity "could only be guaranteed . . . by the presence of a uniform, repressive, and centralized structure, such as governmental practices of the Dutch empire or the New Order" (Lay 2016: 8, my translation).[3] Cornelis Lay, a well-known political actor and observer, identified claims for local autonomy not as motivated by desires for independence from the nation, but for rights of representation and the redress of grievances within the national framework.

Focal in these regional dynamics were towns which had grown rapidly during the New Order era. Broad similarities between those dynamics have allowed them to be identified now as parts of "Middle Indonesia" (van Klinken 2014a, 2014b; van Klinken and Berenschot 2014). "Middle Indonesia" is a rubric that helps recognize that these urban locales, otherwise distant and different from each other, have become "intermediate spaces" for an "intermediate class" of Indonesian citizens. Since the New Order's fall they became sites for new "patterns of political practice" (Lay 2016: 9).[4] They are places where broadly similar "confrontations over class, identity, and other struggles converge and create the potential for progress and integration" (Lay 2016: 9).[5] Indonesian is now the common language of local struggles for national progress and integration.

Middle Indonesian towns, with populations of between fifty thousand and a million, were by 2006 homes to half of all Indonesians. Another 30 percent of the population live within their spheres of influence (van Klinken 2014a: 10). As scenes of engagement between their residents, often across multiple lines of difference, Middle Indonesian towns partake of their regional surrounds; they are meeting places between large metropoles and villages, state and citizenry, modern and traditional forms of economic organization, consumer culture and local practices, and so on.

This book describes Indonesian as the language of two Middle Indonesian towns by looking beyond the regime of the standard to recognize instead the plural character it has developed in local versions of the national project.

Chapter 2 describes Indonesian manners of speaking among middle-class residents of Kupang, capital of Indonesia's southeasternmost province, East Nusa Tenggara (Nusa Tenggara Timur, or NTT), 2,000 kilometers east of Jakarta. Chapter 3 describes Indonesian as it is spoken by some of their counterparts in Pontianak, capital of West Kalimantan (Kalimantan Barat, or Kalbar), on the island of Borneo 700 kilometers north of Jakarta.

This effort to locate Indonesian in a dynamic of national development, but also in everyday lives, is oriented to the multivalued paradox it contains, one identified by Goenawan Mohamad ten years after the New Order fell. To celebrate Indonesian this well-known public intellectual directed attention away from the standard language to its Malay antecedents and nonstandard varieties. These he identified not as marginal or substandard, but as integral to the "very valuable paradox" (*paradoks yang sangat berharga*) that Indonesian contains:

> On one hand it can unify, on the other support radicalized diversity. It has for users almost all Indonesian people, but historically it is not a "majority" language.... [I]ts history ... was shaped in thousands of markets in the archipelago. What difference in that process between "foreign" and "native," "low" and "high," "periphery" and "center"? There has never been one. (Goenawan 2008: 5, my translation)[6]

Goenawan's paradox is thematic in this sketch of other-than-standard varieties of Indonesian. It is part also of the linguistic "miracle" that was enabled. but not fully determined, by the state program of development. Speakers of Indonesian (including Goenawan) often describe Indonesians' manners of speaking as *bahasa gado-gado*: "mixed language" or, more closely translated, "salad language." But here I attend to their structural and expressive coherences, together with their situated values in local integrative dynamics. These are otherwise are marginalized or "erased" (Gal and Irvine 2001, 2019) under the regime of the standard.

When Goenawan celebrated this paradox a few nonstandard varieties of Indonesian were already beginning to gain visibility in less censored print and mass media.[7] The visibility of these vernacular varieties attested to the ways Indonesian had in actuality been "stretching to fit the times" (*geliat bahasa selaras jaman*; Moriyama and Budiman 2010; see also Djenar 2012, 2015, 2016, 2020). Goenawan and others thus recognized that Indonesian's values in its nation needed to be reframed by revisiting broader questions about its forms, and so addressing a challange described by van Putten (2010) as "opening up the language" (*bongkar bahasa*).

Officially, however, the regime of the standard has survived as a durable legacy of the New Order. It was renewed, for instance, in 2009 legislation dictating that standard Indonesian be used in all official documents, communication, and a wide range of public venues.[8] A semiofficial document written in 2007 similarly described standard Indonesian's distinctness and autonomy as a matter of "national politics" (*politik nasional*) to be maintained in relation to what I discuss below as ethnoregional languages (*bahasa daérah*) on one hand, and on the other to foreign languages (*bahasa asing*), especially English.[9]

Here Goenawan's paradox is explored through a few of the many ways that Indonesian figures in the transiencies of everyday talk, and as a mediator of interpersonal engagements. The ways these vary between persons, contexts, and communities require a fairly narrow empirical focus, which I introduce here along with the young, educated residents of Kupang and Pontianak discussed in Chapters 2 and 3. Here I first sketch these geographically and historically different towns and show how they, like other urban centers, developed as ideological "blind spots" for the regime of standard Indonesian. Next I introduce them as homes to speakers of different varieties of Malay.

Ideologically, under the regime of the standard, Malay is one of more than 600 languages that are spoken natively by Indonesians. Historically and structurally, Indonesian can count as "the same language" as Malay. This tension, or paradox, helps here to make fairly close comparisons between the ways both languages figure in the lives of residents of Kupang and Pontianak. So too it allow commonalities among their college students—their social positions, language competences, biographies, and aspirations—to serve as background for a contrastive sketch of the kinds of Indonesian they speak.

Together these sketches speak to the broader paradox of Indonesian as a national lingua franca: spoken almost universally but not, as Goenawan puts it, as a "majority" language. I end this chapter by showing why this makes Indonesian seem to be a miracle to some, and "improbable" (Pisani 2014) to others. At issue are assumptions about nativeness—of language competences on one hand, and national identities on the other--which lack fit with "the Indonesian case." To bracket these in following pages, I first explain why for this reason I sometimes describe Indonesian as an unnative rather than a nonnative language. This word is awkward but also useful in sketches of some particulars of the ways Indonesians talk in chapters 2 and 3; it helps generalize from those particulars to the question of how Indonesian enables its speakers' senses of national belonging in Chapter 4.

Indonesia(n)'s Development

Soon after President Sukarno asserted his nation's place in the nonaligned world, early in the Cold War, Indonesia became a theater for covert operations for the Central Intelligence Agency of the United States. With its help factions of the

Indonesian military deposed Sukarno in 1965, destroyed Indonesia's influential Communist Party, and oversaw the massacre of hundreds of thousands of innocent people over six months. This was a bloody signal that the New Order which then took power would brook no opposition to its development agenda.

Support and guidance from Western nations (Simpson 2009) helped the New Order to centralize its power of oversight and ensure Indonesia's territorial integrity (Elson 2008). This gave the otherwise peripheral towns of Kupang and Pontianak new kinds of visibility as capitals of provinces sharing land borders with other nations. When the Portuguese withdrew from their colony of Timor Leste in 1975, Kupang became the staging ground for an invasion of the new nation, followed by years of unsuccessful efforts by the military to quell resistance to its occupation. West Kalimantan shares a border with the Malaysian province of Sarawak, a region which saw earlier, lesser degrees of conflict with other long-term effects on the province and Pontianak.

Key to the New Order agenda of "accelerated modernization and development" were institutions established to disseminate knowledge of Indonesian among members of a largely uneducated, linguistically diverse population.[10] To that end, schools were established by presidential decree across Indonesia with the core purpose of transmitting knowledge of standard Indonesian. In these and other institutions, including the media, standard Indonesian became the language of one-to-many participant frameworks (Goebel 2015): students engaged with teachers, readers exposed to print media, audiences developed for "mass-communicative" events, and so on. Because standard Indonesian was first and foremost a conduit for official, top-down communication to a disenfranchised citizenry, it was easy for this program to prioritize "passive" or "receptive" competences in the language (Goebel 2015: 9).

This far-reaching program made Indonesian what one political scientist called in 1988 "perhaps the most important single ingredient in the shaping of the modern culture" (Liddle 1988: 1). It was instrumental for agents of the state and, through association with visions of modernity, ideologically distinct from other languages spoken in the country. For the same reason persons who "mixed" its forms with other languages represented an "obstacle towards the development of an Indonesian (*Bahasa Indonésia*) which is really mature, i.e., capable of transmitting modern concepts and modern ideas" (Buchori 1994: 28).

Technocrats overseeing the program of language development (*pembangunan bahasa*) adopted metrics and categories from colleagues engaged in the work of economic development (*pembangunan ékonomi*). (Broader discussion of these parallels is found in Gazzola 2014 and Kaplan and Baldauf 1997: 153.) The founder of that program, Takdir Alisjahbana, made this linkage clear by motivating Indonesian as an "optimally efficient tool for the communicative needs of a modern society" (Grijns 1981: 7; see also, for instance, Alisjahbana 1954, 1968, 1976). Abstract criteria of communicative efficiency helped distinguish Indonesian's utility and uniformity; an absence of native exemplars gave it a distinct portability and neutrality.

Indonesian thus gained legitimacy and authority, over and against all of Indonesia's other languages, through what Susan Gal and Kathryn Woolard (2001) call an ideology of *anonymity*, which privileged it as the "vehicle of communication, belonging to no one in particular" and so (in principle) "equally available to all" (Woolard 2016: 7). Metrics of communicative efficiency, and images of impersonal "neutrality," suited Indonesian well for a top-down program of political and economic change like that being prescribed at that time by proponents of so-called Modernization Theory. Standard Indonesian's anonymity aligned also with values attributed more broadly to state-supported, literate languages by Ernest Gellner in "formal, context-liberated use" in modern national societies (1983: 33).[11]

Because it counted as anonymous and impersonal, standard Indonesian could be disseminated as if it stood in the same relation everywhere to diverse native languages, however much they differed structurally or demographically. All counted as similarly subordinate to what Widdowson has called, with reference to International English, a "set of established encoded forms, unchanged into different domains of use" (1997: 139). Indonesian's anonymity was in this way politically salient for the broader regimenting of ethnoregional diversity.

Regimenting Ethnoregions and Their Languages

Ten years before he bore witness to the Indonesian miracle, Fishman proposed a broad typology for large-scale dynamics of social and linguistic change. He generalized from observations Charles Ferguson had made (1959) about what he called diglossic situations, in which distinct but related "high" and "low" language varieties are used. In diglossic societies, as Ferguson described them, "high" language varieties are acquired through engagement with practices and institutions of literacy. Their uses are distinctly authoritative, prestigious, and associated with public contexts of language use. They stand apart from structurally related but socially distinct "low" languages, acquired and used orally and aurally in the more ordinary contexts of everyday life. "High" languages presuppose and are used in relatively circumscribed contexts, but relatively uniform across time and space; "low" languages are more commonly used but more variable across time, contexts, and communities.

Fishman (1967) bracketed issues of historical and structural relatedness between "high" and "low" languages with a functional distinction that could apply to a much wider range of societies. Indonesia's program of language development could be described in his typology as designed to create a bilingual diglossic society by propagating a national "high" literate language.[12] The regime of the standard served to legitimize Indonesian's superordinate position, and to regiment its relation to all of Indonesia's other languages. This relation presupposed an ideological contrast between the anonymity of "high" Indonesian, and "low," natively spoken, ethnoregional languages.

These "low" languages, however different from each other, all counted as distinctively native (*asli*) to their speakers and regions. The word *asli* can be translated as "native," "originary," or *authentic*, using Gal and Woolard's term for the kind of legitimacy languages derive from perceptions that they are "deeply rooted in social and geographic territory" (Woolard 2016: 22). "High" Indonesian's anonymity and portability in this way complemented "low" languages' authenticity and locality.

In this way putatively "natural" connections were officialized between languages, subsets of the national citizenry, and subparts of national territory. The demarcation of native languages, speakers, and territories was carried out with categories inherited from the Netherlands East Indies. Indonesian citizens, like imperial subjects, were understood to have "one—and only one—extremely clear place. No fractions" (Anderson 1991: 166). But for regions to count as discrete and homogeneous, linguistically and culturally,[13] actualities of local difference had to be superceded by official images of languages, cultures, and histories. This kind of quasi-official ideological work can be illustrated with the Javanese, who form by far Indonesia's largest ethnic group (numbering more than 90 million).

The prototypical "Javanese" (*orang Jawa*) is a native speaker of Javanese (*penutur asli bahasa Jawa*) and native or ancestrally connected to regions of the island of Java (*tanah Jawa*), primarily the provinces of Central Java and East Java, but also Banten on the west coast. In fact millions of persons who count as Javanese have been born and grown up in other parts of the country for more than a century, many as native speakers of other languages. Relevant here, however, are 70 million Javanese who live in these regions but in reality speak several distinct "dialects" of Javanese, not all mutually intelligible (Conners and Van der Klok 2016; Arps 2010; Kisyani-Laksono 2011).

Under the New Order such regional and cultural differences in Javanese regions were residualized, superseded, or erased with quasi-official, emblematic representations of a common language, culture, and history. This involved visions of a deep ethnic heritage, partly taken over from Dutch scholars, which allowed images of Javaneseness to be tied to descendants of nobility living in south-central regions of the island. Their exemplary status was marked crucially by fluency in "polished" styles of Javanese speech which most Javanese have little opportunity to learn or occasion to use (Errington 1998b, Widodo 2017).

Under the diglossic regime, talk that "mixes" elements of Indonesian and ethnoregional languages counts as structurally interstitial and ideologically marginal. But it has been commonplace enough in Java, as elsewhere, that the phrase used to describe it in Indonesian—and by Goenawan Mohamad to title the essay quoted above--was borrowed from Javanese.[14]

This book is about a few such local realities, and the ways they diverge both markedly and meaningfully from the diglossic regime on one hand, and ethnoregional norms on the other. Chapter 3, for instance, discusses persons who identify ethnically as "Dayak" but speak different native languages, and others who are extremely fluent speakers of Indonesians but of Chinese descent, and so without a native ethnoregion. These are just some of the clearest examples of the ways Middle Indonesian towns have become not just regional centers of national modernity, but exceptions to the ethnoregional rule.

Urban Centers and Their Vernaculars

For most Indonesians, Jakarta has long been not just the nation's capital but the paradigm of modernity. Founded as the Dutch settlement of Batavia in 1619, it became capital of the Netherlands East Indies and the site of what John Furnivall (1944) described as a "plural economy." He coined this phrase to foreground the segregated character of life among Batavia's residents, where differences of race extended to economic roles, places of residence, manners of life, native languages, and so on. But urban life and the imperial economy nonetheless required linguistic means for bridging those differences, if only for specific, practical purposes. These needs were met with varieties of Malay, many spoken nonnatively, that came to be known collectively by the city's name: *bahasa Betawi* before independence, and *bahasa Jakarta* after.[15]

This variety of Malay is now widely recognized to be the language of the "special region of the capital" (*daérah istiméwa ibukota*), but also as an exception to the ethnoregional rule. This condition was quite clear to officials who established the Center for Language Improvement and Development (*Pusat Pembinaan dan Pengembangan Bahasa*). Anton Moeliono, a leading figure in that office, suggested during a television broadcast in the 1970s that the "language of Jakarta" could eventually serve analogous roles in Indonesia's other rapidly growing, ethnically diverse cities. To this end, he identified Jakartan Malay as an "informal variety of standard Indonesian"—*bahasa Indonésia baku laras informal* (Oetomo 1996: 200)—and the "Jakartan dialect of Indonesian" (*bahasa Indonésia dialèk Jakarta*).

By renaming a centuries-old dialect of Malay Moeliono made it standard Indonesian's stylistic complement and the everyday language of urban modernity in the "hub that mattered most" (Goebel, Cole, and Manns 2020: 5). It provided, in Moeliono's view, a fitting linguistic response to needs resulting from urban dynamics that were distant but overseen from the capital.

Now Jakarta's vernacular is widely recognized in large part because it circulates in various mass and digital media. But Moeliono's prediction that it would spread as a spoken complement to standard Indonesian has not proven correct. Even in towns relatively close to Jakarta, like Malang in eastern Java, the "Jakarta variety [of Indonesian] is not viewed positively in all situations" (Musgrave 2014: 100; see also Manns 2014).[16] Beyond the capital's ambit, Jakartan manners of speaking circulating through one-to-many participation frameworks have taken on ambiguous values and variable uses (Manns 2014, 2019; Manns et al. 2020).

Middle Indonesian towns served the New Order as regional centers for the state bureaucracy, as points of entry for capital and technology, and as nodes in expanding infrastructures of mobility (Muhidin 2014; Carruthers 2017a). They became more distinct from but also more accessible for persons living in their provincial surrounds; growing numbers of newcomers made them scenes of encounter between more persons of different ethnic and linguistic backgrounds.

Linguistic correlates of these developments in Middle Indonesian towns, including Kupang and Pontianak, have made them homes to other-than-standard Indonesians similar to what Moeliono identified as Jakarta's informal variety of Indonesian. Like Jakarta's Malay, they are spoken natively by some residents, but not others who have come to these cities later in life, primarily from their provincial surrounds. These urban centers figure in a dynamic of "redistributed centralization" or what might be appear in the nation's capital as a "multi-centered peripherality" (Goebel, Cole, and Manns 2020: 5). These manners of speaking reflect centripetal forces emanating from Jakarta, but also centrifugal forces exerted by the presence of residents from their respective peripheries.

So different "mixtures" of Malay and Indonesian spoken in urban centers, although they violate the regime of the standard, can serve, like Jakarta's, as its complements. Their forms can be described relative to social values they have as linguistic means for "negotiating" or "softening" the kinds of tensions Lay (2016: 9) identified as accompanying new class formations, transitions between traditional practices and a consumer culture, and more.[17]

Cities and Students

In 2011, the last year of research I draw on here, about five million young Indonesians were enrolled in institutions of higher education (*perguruan tinggi*).[18] As they came of age in an era of reform they negotiated paths through a national educational hierarchy with the means to become college students, or *mahasiswa*.

However different their biographies and ethnoregional backgrounds, *mahasiswa* form a distinct segment of Indonesia's youth (*anak muda*). They are at the threshold of adulthood, and many seek academic credentials as means of entry to secure, middle class employment as civil servants (*PNS, pegawai nasional sipil*). They inherit at the same time a tradition of political activism long associated with Indonesian youth (*pemuda* and *pemudi*) which the New Order succeeded in neutralizing only temporarily. This heritage is commemorated yearly in re-enactments of the proclamation of loyalty on October 18, 1928, famous as the "Pledge of the Youth" (*Sumpah Pemuda*), to the Indonesian nation, people, and language.

Mahasiswa are among the least directly supervised members of a "cosmopolitan, Indonesian youth culture" (Smith-Hefner 2007: 184) that includes adolescents (*anak baru gedé*) and teenagers (*orang remaja*). Indonesian youth, particularly in cities, are broadly associated with "new types of social identifications through the formulation of relationships that are more egalitarian and interactionally fluid" (Smith-Hefner 2007: 184). These identifications and images of youth can be enacted and recognized, in turn, with styles of speech called *bahasa gaul*, translatable as the "language of sociability." *Bahasa gaul* has values for these youths, like manners of speech among youths in England described by Ben Rampton, as expressions of their "non-canonical positioning" in urban society (2011: 289).

Anxieties about Indonesian youth are often projected onto this "language of sociability" as spoken in Jakarta. It circulates, like Jakarta's vernacular more broadly, through one-to-many participation frameworks, and as a resource for group dynamics among young Indonesians elsewhere, along with other urban vernaculars, ethnoregional languages, and English (see Manns 2014, 2019). College students acquire local varieties of *bahasa gaul* as means for enacting broadly "anti-normative" stances to "perceived rigid traditions and hierarchies" (Djenar, Ewing, and Manns 2018: 28). Yet their biographies and aspirations reflect also their deep engagement with the nation's institutional hierarchies.

These vernacular manners of speech thus indirectly reflect what Nakassis calls, in the case of their counterparts in Tamil Nadu, "multiple and contested" places in urban life that *mahasiswa* "only ever inhabit [. . .] in partial ways" (2013: 248). They help distinguish members of what Wenty Minza calls, relative to Pontianak, "cultures of educated youth" (2014a: 132). *Mahasiswa* are seen and see themselves as engaged with spheres of modernity which extend beyond their towns and provinces, thanks in part to language competences—in standard Indonesian, but also English—that mark them as members of an educated middle-class citizenry.

The visibility of *mahasiswa* extends to lifestyles—*gaya mahasiswa*—that are emulated by age-mates who are unable or unwilling to become students themselves (Minza 2014a: 131–146; see also Minza 2014b). Their ways of dressing, associating with others, and patterns of consumption cohere in images of "the college student" that are meaningful not just in educational institutions but scenes of urban life generally. Occupants of the category "college student" can enact and be perceived as "embodied symbols of the promise and problems of new economic realities." (Wilson 2004: 191). Their modes of conduct, verbal and otherwise, can allow them in this way to enact what Joshua Barker and colleagues (2013) call a distinct "figure of modernity," that is, an image of personhood associated broadly with the modern nation, but instantiated or enacted against the ground of everyday urban life.

In this context other-than-standard ways of speaking Indonesian can be seen as integral for the ways *mahasiswa* find places in and adopt stances to city life, particularly when interacting with each other. They can be seen also as exemplars of another paradox: they are highly educated Indonesians who routinely flout the regime of the standard language.

Student Backgrounds, Biographies, and Communities

The presence of newcomers in Middle Indonesian towns serve to integrate them with their rural surrounds, and this geosocial relation has an everyday relevance that can be illustrated with another use of the word *daérah*. Besides serving to designate subparts of the nation (*negara*) and their languages (*bahasa daérah*), it can be used to identify places, communities, and persons that are outside but proximate to cities (*kota*), more like "(part of a) regional surround." A college student in Pontianak can identify a group of classmates, for instance, as being from (i.e., having come of age in) the *daérah*, that is, various rural parts of West Kalimantan. A student in Kupang, asked about her roommate's whereabouts said in a similar manner "she went to the *daérah*," that is, to one or another rural place beyond the city but within its purview (in this case, for a visit "back home").

This means that biographical differences are easily identified between *mahasiswa* who came of age as urban natives, and those who are newcomers, later in life, from the regions. These differences extend to the social circumstances in which they acquire competences in Indonesian even as they progress through the same national educational system. In more rural, less modern communities, the diglossic regime of the standard can shape stronger senses of the contrast between "high" literate Indonesian and distinct "low" ethnoregional languages; this carries over into widespread stereotypes associating lack of fluency in standard Indonesian with poor, rural segments of society (Goebel 2015: 101).

In towns like Kupang and Pontianak, on the other hand, young persons acquire competences in Indonesian with weaker practical senses of the "high" language's distinctness from the "low" manners of speaking that are appropriate outside institutional settings. In these urban milieux, as Moeliono suggested for Jakarta, the regime of the standard lacks purchase on differences not between national and ethnoregional languages, but the standard and informal styles of speech.

So newcomers from surrounding regions find that their fluency in standard Indonesian is not sufficient to deal with the challenges of urban life. So they seek to acquire facility, on the fly, in vernacular manners of speech needed for routine interaction in the city, especially with peers. In this way the biographies of *mahasiswa* are an important theme in this book for identifying different ways Indonesian is spoken and valued in urban life generally, including the manners of speaking that allow members of the category "educated youth" to form distinctive *communities of practice*.

The concept of community of practice helps to link fine-grained features of verbal events to interactionally grounded senses of mutuality and identity. In chapters 2 and 3 this involves the ways Indonesians spoken by young persons in Kupang and Pontianak, standard and otherwise, are part of their "com[ing] together around mutual engagement in an endeavor. Ways of doing things, ways of talk, beliefs, values, power relations—in short, practices—emerge in the course of this mutual endeavor" (Eckert and McConnell-Ginet 1992: 464).

The "ways of talk" that distinguish and enable such engagements can be identified, in turn, as instances of *registers* of speech, that is, as having features which are recognized to be linked, implicitly or overtly, to "interactionally relevant personae and models of action" (Agha 2007: 55). The term register is important here to describe the ways that structurally "mixed speech" among *mahasiswa* can be expressively coherent relative to "cultural images of persons as well as situations and activities" (Irvine 1990: 127). For young, educated Indonesians these images extend more broadly to their "jointly constructed beliefs, values, and orientations to society" (Eckert and McConnell-Ginet 1992: 490).

Indonesian and/as Malay

Structurally mixed, expressively coherent registers of "mixed" speech, or "colloquial Indonesian" (Ewing 2005), are an urban commonplace. To describe their places in everyday life, and explore Goenawan's paradox, I take advantage of the fact that Kupang and Pontianak are both homes to speakers of Malay. Malay counts as standard Indonesian's antecedent, which is why historical connections and structural similarities between them are important here for showing how and why talk so commonly lacks conformance with the regime of the standard.

The phrase "Malay language" (*bahasa Melayu*) itself applies to many different ways of speaking and writing. Some bear the names of cities where they are spoken (like *bahasa Jakarta* and *bahasa Kupang*). Some are dialects of an ethnic language native to regions of coastal Kalimantan, Sumatra, and the Malay peninsula; among these is the variety spoken in and around Pontianak (*bahasa Melayu Pontianak*). Still others, indirectly identified by Goenawan with "thousands of markets in all the islands of Indonesia," are lingua franca varieties of Malay.

Europeans first encountered lingua franca varieties of Malay along trade routes between the Indian Ocean, coastal Southeast Asia, and the Indonesian archipelago. They acquired these in encounters with persons of many different backgrounds, for a wide range of military, mercantile, and (eventually) missionizing interests:

> [D]erived from many nations, each according to its own language and tongue, and . . . sometimes mixed with some words from Portuguese, or from any other language for that matter . . . it also has the name *Bahasa Kastjoekan*, that is, mixed language, or *Bahasa Pasar*, that is, market language, insofar as it is the language used by merchants who are trading with one another on the market to make things clear and to understand each other. (Francois Valentijn [1724–1726], quoted by H. M. J. Maier 2004: 9)

"Low" Malays served situated, transactional purposes for persons who shared no other language competences, and little concern for "interference" or "transfer" effects from their native languages. They stood apart, in a diglossic manner, from "high" Malay which was learned and used by literate elites who were versed in Arabic and the Islamic faith.

At that time, persons who counted as Malays (*orang Melayu*) were known more by their Islamic faith and fealty to sultans than by their language or region.[19] After the Portuguese defeated the Sultan of Melaka in 1511 a Malay diaspora and pattern of coastal migration eventually led to the founding of Pontianak in 1771, under the leadership of a Hadramaut Arab, at the confluence of the Landak and Kapuas rivers on Borneo's west coast. I outline in Chapter 3 its early development into a plural society of rigidly segregated Chinese and Malay communities.

Kupang was founded in 1653 as a Dutch fort and trading center on the western end of Timor to control Portuguese ambitions in the area. Like Batavia, it became a scene of encounter between persons of many different backgrounds who had recourse to "low" Malay as a highly variable lingua franca. Children coming of age there elaborated, regularized, and nativized creole varieties of Malay, the antecedents of what became over three centuries the language spoken by the town's natives, and acquired later in life by newcomers from surrounding islands and regions.[20]

Kupang's importance for the Dutch declined along with their concerns about the Portuguese presence, and the value of the sandalwood trade. As the empire grew, Kupang became an administrative backwater while Pontianak gained importance as a point of access to the interior of Borneo. Batavia, only slightly older than Kupang, likewise became home to native speakers of diverse languages, and to creole varieties of Malay similar to Kupang's. But unruly varieties of *bahasa Betawi* which served the needs of everyday life (Maier 1993) could not meet those of imperial offices or agents.[21] By the late nineteenth century, the workings of the government were hampered by the lack of such a language on one hand, and on the other Dutch reluctance to educate their native subordinates ("*inlanders*") in their own. Officials on either side of the imperial divide had recourse instead to "low" or pidginized varieties of what was known euphemistically as "service Malay" *(dienst Maleisch)* or more critically as "babbling" *(brabbeltaal)*.[22]

By the turn of the century this condition was untenable enough that the imperial government took steps to codify and propagate an official, literate variety of Malay. Charles Van Ophuisen was given responsibility for producing what he called "general, polished Malay" *(algemeen beschaafd Maleisch)*, a literate register partly devised and partly modeled on speech among Malay natives of the Riau Islands (then a British possession located between the coasts of Sumatra and Malaya).[23] Thanks to an "extraordinary symbiosis of scholarship with the metropolitan politics of a colonizing state" (Hoffman 1979: 74) this variety of Malay became a language that acquired by students at imperial schools. A proprietary attitude toward "general, polished Malay" may have prevented the Dutch from seeing that members of their subaltern elite (including the youth, or *pemuda*) could turn it to other purposes.[24]

Benedict Anderson observed the crucial role that this Malay had for the ethnically and linguistically diverse group of literates who sought to negotiate their political and social marginality as members of "native society" who were also colonial administrators poised "precariously over diverse monoglot populations" (1991: 114). Indonesian's value for their vision of a nation was, in his words, like that of the eye for a lover (1991: 154).

Two generations later, Pramoedya Ananta Toer, a young journalist who was to become the leading literary figure of his generation, gave a series of lectures about what he called the "prehistory" *(prasedjarah)* of Indonesian, looking beyond what he called the "school Malay" (*Melayu-sekolah*) of those "educated to become civil servants" (1963a).[25] Crucial for him, as for Goenawan, were Indonesian's roots in what he called "working languages" (*basa kerdja*) which varied as much as the groups that fashioned them, and the practical, objective, local needs it met (1963b).[26]

Pramoedya chose these labels to avoid the feudal (*féodal*) distinction between "high Malay," on the one hand, and "low," "market," or "mixed" Malay, on the other. This served his Marxist vision of a future in which all registers of the language would fuse in a classless national society. But as a prominent leftist intellectual he became a target for the New Order, which arrested and threw him into internal exile for 33 years. His "school language" became the New Order's "good and true Indonesian" (*bahasa Indonésia yang baik dan benar*). Under the regime of the standard "low" vernacular registers of Malay became more marginal than the languages of the ethnoregions.

Pramoedya, like Goenawan, celebrated a plurality of Indonesians beyond literate registers acquired by those "being educated to become civil servants." The work of national language development, on the other hand, residualized ways of speaking Indonesian which the regime of the standard did not fully govern. To describe connections between them requires attention to points of structural congruence and difference between "high" national Indonesian and "low" local varieties of Malay.

For this reason I focus here on what Kathryn Woolard calls *bivalent* elements of Indonesian and Malay, that is, linguistic forms that can be classified as belonging "equally, descriptively and even prescriptively, to both languages" (1999: 7). Bivalent elements are relevant here because they elude the regime of the standard, figuring in "mixed" use similar to that Woolard has described among bilingual speakers of Catalan and Castillian.

The social expressiveness of these registers of speech can also be described as deriving from their *syncretic* character.[27] I adopt this term, as did Woolard, from Jane and Kenneth Hill's description (1986) of speech among Mexican peasants in which elements of two languages—Spanish (Castillian) and Mexicano (Nahuatl)—figure together. Under "certain determined conditions" the structurally "mixed" character of such talk has no particular social salience.[28] Identifying syncretic features here helps to bracket and avoid awkward labels like "bidialectal" and "biaccentual."

Bivalent forms and syncretic structures are thematic for empirical sketches of other-than-standard Indonesians in Chapters 2 and 3, and their relations to contexts of use and biographies of users. They are also important for locating nonstandard Indonesians in the broader paradox of a national lingua franca.

Indonesian as an Unnative Language

To classify Indonesian as a lingua franca is to tacitly liken it to the original "language of the Franks," which served communicative needs between Arabs and Europeans along the Mediterranean coast between the fourteenth and eighteenth centuries. That lingua franca was, as one linguist put it, "barely a language at all" (Schuchardt 1979: 27). But the same label can be used to liken Indonesian to various literate languages used over centuries to enable communication between literate elites, in the absence of another common language. Among these are Sanskrit, Latin, Arabic, and now global English.

"Lingua franca" can be used so broadly, like "vehicular language" and "language of wider communication," because it has a negative semantic valence: it identifies languages which, however different otherwise, lack native speakers, either categorically (as in the case of standard Indonesian) or contextually (as in the case of global English).[29] This use tacitly presupposes divergence from a condition of linguistic nativeness which is natural in that it develops as a property of individuals during what linguists call the critical period for language acquisition. One's native language ("first language," or "mother tongue")[30] is acquired before puberty, and is inalienable in the sense that it can exert "interference" or "transfer" effects on other linguistic abilities acquired later in life in a "second" or "foreign" language.

Knowledge of a lingua franca stands apart from that of other languages, then, as a nonnative language competence. But the category "native language" serves not just to identify individuals' linguistic abilities, but their membership in social groups. This occurs when persons identified as native speakers of the same language are aggregated by criteria other than language competence. An example noted earlier was the designation of Javanese as officially native for millions, although its emblematic forms are "native" to only a tiny fraction of that group. This illustrates the naturalizing effects which use of the category "native language" can have when applied to persons whose manners of speaking nonetheless differ.

Alignments between images of national languages and literate registers of language can cohere in images of native "best speakerhood" (Silverstein 1996: 286) which can be powerful naturalizers of hierarchy in monoglot national societies.[31] Stephanie Hackert (2012) describes such a development among speakers of English in nineteenth-century England. Philological images of an older, purer state of the language became a means for categorizing expanding numbers of speakers and varieties of English. Literacy-centered images of an "authentic" English became associated with habits of speech acquired among elites, naturalizing their statuses as exemplary native speakers. Their native manners of speaking could be positioned as "natural" reference points for judging others, and their "native" speakers, as different but also deficient ("accented," "dialectal," "ungram-matical," "illogical," and so on).

Forms of English are used by Indonesians as another lingua franca that figures regularly in the kinds of talk I discuss here. I suggest that the anonymity it shares with standard Indonesian enables easy recourse to global (not foreign) English in otherwise vernacular talk. Fashions of speaking sketched in Chapters 2 and 3 illustrate this commonality with Indonesian as a national language which, to borrow Widdowson's observation on International English (EIL), is a body of conventions that can be "variously actualized . . . by communities adapting it to their changing needs" (1997: 142).

The emergence of global English itself produced controversy centered on the category "native speaker." In the late 1990s (see for instance Singh 1998) some parties contested and others defended use of this label for persons who acquired their competences while coming of age in South Asia. Objections were raised not on the basis of their fluency or intelligibility, but historical (and crypto-racial) relations between the United Kingdom and its former settlement colonies on one hand, and its former exploitation colonies on the other.

Peter Muyskens (1998) pointedly identified the ideological grounds for this debate, and ideas of linguistic nativeness generally, by observing we are all native speakers and asking "but what language are we native speakers of?" His rhetorical question foregrounds the social grounds for this mode of characterization, and indirectly the slippage it enables between literate and oral varieties of language.

The absence of "natural" linkage between letter and voice is a distinguishing character of Indonesian which posed a pedagogical problem early in its devel-opment: who could serve as a proper model for the spoken language (*ragam ujar*)? Some wished to accord that status to an exemplary individual, President Sukarno, a native speaker of Javanese whose abilities in Indonesian had made him the "extension of the tongue of the people" (*penyambung lidah rakyat*). Others proposed that a panel of literary figures establish a standard for pronunciation. In 1974, writing with the benefit of hindsight, the noted pedagogue I Gusti Ngurah Oka observed that because such proposals were not practical, teachers should be shown how to exercise (what he referred to in English as) "common sense" (and translated into Indonesian as *perasaan umum*; 1974: 131). Masnur Muslich echoed his recommendation (2010: 250) as still appropriate in the era of globalization.

The practical problem at issue was the universality of transfer or "interfer-ence" effects into standard Indonesian from Indonesians' native habits of speech. These include features of pronunciation (accent), the grammatical elements used to create words and order phrases, intonational contours that convey affect and informational relevance, particles marking expressive stances, and so on. All vary as do Indonesians' native languages, which is why Indonesian can only transcend the nation's linguistic heterogeneity by partly reproducing it. The upshot, as pedagogues recognized early on, is that Indonesians were not just learning but "creating many kinds of Indonesian" (Lindsay 2006, 2013).

Benedict Anderson observed in the 1980s that "perhaps millions of young Indonesians, from dozens of ethnolinguistic backgrounds, . . . speak Indonesian as their mother-tongue" (1991: 134). But he passed over the diversity of habits of speech that carry over from other languages. Most can be called native speakers of Indonesian only if they are further recognized to be, as one young Javanese described himself in English, "natively bilingual" (quoted in Kozok 2016).

To discuss consequences of this disjunction between "standard Indonesian" and "native Indonesian" it helps sometimes to describe it as "unnative." This term is useful, if awkward, for avoiding assumptions or habits of thought that lack fit with "the Indonesian case" but that the commoner "nonnative" does not disallow. This is because the meaning of "nonnative" is what logicians call contradictory to that of its root. What can be called "nonnative" or "nonmilitary," for instance, lacks properties that some other entities possess (nativeness or militariness). For that reason such constructions often align semantically with synonyms: what is "nonnative" can usually be described also as "foreign" or "alien;" what is "nonmilitary" is "civilian," and so on. To describe standard Indonesian forms, uses, or speakers as "nonnative" would similarly and falsely presuppose that they can identified through features they lack and others have.

"Unnative" is semantically contrary to "native": it identifies what is beyond, inimical to, or entirely skewed with whatever possess qualities of nativeness. The meaning of "unmilitary" for this reason differs from that of "civilian" because it identifies things not as lacking an attribute that others possess, but as being entirely different from, skewed with, or opposed to the sphere of militariness. For the same reason "unnative" is useful here for discussing Indonesian forms, speech, and speakers in the absence of native exemplars.[32]

Under the regime of the standard, Indonesian's unnativeness is the source of what Keane calls the standard language's "alterity" (2003: 514). Relative to everyday talk, on the other hand, an absence of instances or images of native speakership enables floutings of that regime. Chapter 4 reviews examples of such syncretic talk to show how that unnativeness may be a feature, not a bug, of the Indonesian linguistic "miracle."

Unity and Plurality

Sketches of other-than-standard Indonesians provide a "bottom-up" perspective on Goenawan's paradox, and unnative Indonesian's role in its speakers' senses of national commonality. "Mixed use" is framed here as a site of a productive tension, or ambiguity, not between "high" and "low" languages, but senses of membership in a national citizenry and communities of practice.

In Chapter 4, I generalize from sketches of Kupang and Pontianak by aligning them with a darker side of the "Indonesian miracle": the threat it now poses to many ethnoregional languages. These dynamics of language shift are more visible than those sketched in Chapters 2 and 3, but help to locate them in the broader condition of linguistic plurality. Then I consider other-than-standard Indonesians as they figure in their speakers' ambient awarenesses of others as sharers of a unified, unifying national language. Anderson's influential account of nationalism helps here to link unnative Indonesian to imaginings, as he calls them, of an otherwise anonymous national citizenry. So too interactional events discussed in Chapters 2 and 3 can be reviewed as sources of "cultural intimacy," or sentiments of national belonging, as described by Michael Herzfeld. I suggest that in these transient events speakers may share senses of what he calls "external embarrassment" (1997: 172) relative to absent, anonymous speakers of "the same" national language. Herzfeld helps in this way to look beyond the diglossic regime to the kinds of talk that can mark the local within the national.

This account of Indonesian's development, unlike that celebrated by Fishman in 1978, is not about a Third World nation emulating the modernity of nations in the First World. It is situated in an era of globalization, when Indonesia's linguistic heterogeneity seems to be developing analogs elsewhere. So Indonesian's plurality is worth comparing with sociolinguistic dynamics that are now commoner, or at least more visible, in the Global North. Then this fairly fine-grained sketch of integrative dynamics might offer "insight into the workings of the world at large" (Comaroff and Comaroff 2012b: 114), and a model for newer, "nationally imagined communities of difference" (2012a: 75).

Notes

1. Census data from 1945 indicate that before the program of language development, very few of the 70 million Indonesians knew Indonesian. Data assembled by A. Na'im and H. Syaputra for the Center for Statistics in 2010 indicate that 92 percent of 240 million Indonesians now have competence in the language. On the difficulties of evaluating data from the 1971, 1980, and 1990 censuses see Steinhauer (1994) and Musgrave (2014). See also Kozok (2016) on data from the 2010 census. For a review of census data in the context of educational policy, see Zein (2020). These data are evidence of long-term, cumulative linguistic change in Indonesian society, but drawn from ambiguous responses to oversimple queries, as Chapters 2 and 3 show.

2. Indonesian territory consists of 17,000 islands spanning about 1,800 miles of the equator. Among its current population of about 260 million are speakers of more than 700 native languages.

3. ". . . [M]erupakan pembalikan sangat fundamental atas kesimpulan umum yang sudah menahun di Indonésia: Indonésia yang bersatu hanya bisa dijamin melalui . . . kehadiran sebuah struktur yang seragam-represif-sèntralistis sebagaimana didèmonstrasikan melalui baik corak memerintah Kolonial Belanda maupun Orde Baru" (2016: 8).

4. "[L]etak kekuatan yang mempertemukan keberagaman Indonésia adalah pada 'middle Indonesia' yang didèfinisikan secara longgar sebagai ruang antara, kelas antara, sekaligus usia yang memiliki corak praktis politik sehari-hari yang khas pula."

5. "[D]imana pergulatan kelas, identitas dan anéka perjuangan lainnya menyatu dan membèntuk kekuatan bagi kemajuan dan sekaligus intègrasi."

6. "Maka bahasa Indonésia mengandung paradoks yang sangat berharga. Di satu pihak ia bisa mempersatukan, di lain pihak ia mendukung radikalisasi kebhinékaan. Dari penggunanya bahasa ini dipakai hampir semua orang Indonésia, tapi dari sejarahanya ia bukan bahasa 'mayoritas'. . . . [S]ejarahnya . . . dibèntuk di ribuan pasar di Nusantara. Dalam prosès itu, apa béda antara 'asing' dan 'asli', 'rendah' dan 'tinggi', 'pinggir' dan 'pusat'? Tak pernah ada." Also available at http://web.archive.org/web/20130305101458/http://goenawanmohamad.com/2010/01/16/gado-gado/, accessed January 5, 2020.

7. Such use of Indonesian, particularly with Javanese and Sundanese, has been described by Arps (2010); Cole (2010, 2014); Goebel (2015, 2017); Goebel, Cole, and Manns (2014, 2020); Jurriëns (2009); Manns (2019); Manns, Cole, and Goebel (2020); and Martin-Anatias (2018a, 2018b).

8. For further discussion, see Zentz (2015) and van der Putten (2012).

9. I paraphrase here an unpublished paper written for the Language Bureau (*Pusat Bahasa*): "Seharusnya, bangsa Indonésia menempatkan bahasa Indonésia, bahasa daérah, dan bahasa asing pada posisinya masing-masing sesuai dèngan kedudukan dan fungsinya sebagaimana dinyatakan dalam politik nasional." See Zentz (2017: 76–79) on the legal framing of this relation (Kementerian Pendidikan Nasional 2009).

10. For a broad overview, see Nababan (1991).

11. For a critical review of language development under the New Order, see Heryanto (1987, 1989, 1990, and 2007). For discussion of Gellner's modernist/economistic theory of nationalism and national languages, see Errington (1998a, 1998b).

12. For discussion of diglossia in Indonesia, see Sneddon (2003a, 2003b).

13. My use of "ethnoregional" is suggested by Tom Boellstorff's discussion of the "ethnolocal" (2002, 2005), but is more helpful when dealing with the urban/rural relations which are a key concern here. Goebel (2015 and 2017) discusses the colonial origins of these connections and their vicissitudes in the national era.

14. For more on Javanese and Indonesian usage, see Errington (1998b); Goebel (2002, 2008, 2009, 2010a, 2010b); and Tamtamo (2016, 2017, 2018a, and 2018b).

15. *Bahasa Betawi* applies more narrowly to a creole Malay once spoken natively by descendants of a community present at the time of Batavia's founding, but now is used more broadly like *bahasa Jakarta*. On koinéized vernacular varieties, see Grijns (1981); Sneddon (2002, 2006).

16. See, in this vein, observations by Anthony Jukes (2015) on Makassar and Manado Malay in their respective regions of Sulawesi.

17. " '[M]iddle Indonesia' memainkan péran bukan saja sebagai penghubung tapi sekaligus menjalankan fungsi 'negosiasi' berikut fungsi 'melunakkan' anéka ketegangan yang dihasilkan baik melalui prosès ékonomi seperti kelas, maupun prosès kebudayaan—tradisional vs modèrnitas—atau identitas."

18. See https://databoks.katadata.co.id/datapublish/2019/09/26/tertinggi-sejak-1997-jumlah-mahasiswa-indonesia-2018-capai-7-juta-jiwa, accessed January 26, 2020.

19. Two different views on the origins and history of Malay can be found in Adelaar (2004) and Collins (2004). For discussions of Malay as a national and ethnic category, see Barnard (2004) and Long (2013).

20. Jacob (2014) provides a general account of Kupang Malay as a creole. Paauw (2008) provides comparative evidence for an alternative account of Kupang Malay as one of several varieties with origins in a single widely used Eastern Indonesia Trade Malay (EITM).

21. For a broad account of the history of Malay, see Collins (1998). On Malay as a language of early Dutch colonialism, see Hoffman (1973). For discussion of Indonesian in relation to Riau Malay language, see Gil (2010); Maier (2004).

22. See Grijns (1996) and Errington (2008).

23. Edisruslan Pe Amarinza (2001) discusses Riau Malay's relation to standard Indonesian early in the post–New Order era. For a valuable review of and corrective to more recent, widespread, negative views of Riau Malay, see Gil (2010).

24. Summaries of this process and relevant sources are in Collins (1998) and Errington (2008).

25. "[B]asa-sekolah hanja berlaku bagi mereka jang dididik mendjadi hamba pemerintah, para ambtenar, terutama para guru, pemupuk benih2 birokrat."

26. "Basa kerdja itu tumbuh disebabkan kebutuhan sosial jang objectif."

27. Discussion and further examples involving Indonesian and Javanese are in Errington (1998b).

28. The Hills adapted the term "syncretic" from work by the Indo-European linguist Jerzy Kurylowicz (1964).

29. See, e.g., Mauranen (2018).

30. See also Bonfiglio's philological (2010) and Seidler's ethnographic (2009) commentaries on the category "mother tongue."

31. Parallel observations on governmentality and "mother tongues" can be found in Pennycook (2002) and Wright (2003).

32. Its awkwardness, largely a matter of connotation, arises from the ways that the construction maps evaluative negativity on semantic negativity. This point, made by Otto Jespersen (1942), is discussed at length by Larry Horn (2001).

2 A PROVINCIAL INDONESIAN

Nusa Tenggara Tengah (NTT) is among the least developed of Indonesia's provinces. Infant mortality, food insecurity, and the number of residents living below the national poverty line (van Klinken 2014b: 263) all reflect a paucity of commodifiable resources, fertile soil, and reliable rainfall on the province's 500 islands. NTT's remoteness can be inferred from the fact that its five million citizens make up less than 2 percent of Indonesia's population but speak 10 percent of its ethnoregional languages. They are also marginal religiously as predominantly Christian members of an overwhelmingly Muslim national citizenry.[1]

Viewed from elsewhere in Indonesia, Kupang might seem a distant administrative backwater. But when it became logistically important for the New Order's invasion of Timor Leste in 1975, it became also the center of a burgeoning bureaucracy and home to cadres of civil servants (*pegawai negeri sipil*, PNS), who form the largest part of Kupang's educated middle class. Identifying them as members of a political class—as does Sylvia Tidey (2012: 8), following Jacqueline Vel's use of the term (2008) elsewhere in NTT—helps to keep in mind their multiple affiliations with institutions of the state.

It would be easy to assume that these affiliations would be evident from competence in and frequent use of "good and true" Indonesian. In practice, though, standard Indonesian is not routinely used among even the most educated members of Kupang's political class. Instead, they combine elements of Indonesian with *bahasa Kupang*, the creole Malay introduced in Chapter 1. This gives rise to the paradox, observed by Barbara Grimes (2005), that "bad Indonesian" can be "good Kupang Malay." I explore it here among young persons whose biographies and aspirations align with knowledge of standard Indonesian, but whose habits of speech regularly incorporate Kupang's "ignored and despised" vernacular (Jacob and Grimes 2006).

This paradox can be situated socially and biographically by first considering different ways that *mahasiswa*, as aspiring members of NTT's political class, acquire standard Indonesian and Kupang's

Other Indonesians. Joseph Errington, Oxford University Press. © Oxford University Press 2022.
DOI: 10.1093/oso/9780197563670.003.0002

vernacular. Then I sketch similarities between their habits of talk, showing how these are more expressively coherent and syncretic, rather than structurally interstitial between "high" Indonesian and "low" Malay. A few specifics are presented first to demonstrate how Indonesian's unnativeness, and the unethnic character of Kupang's vernacular, enable educated urbanites' ways of speaking. They illustrate also structural regularities of talk when the language of the nation figures in a local variety of Malay. Then the ideological ambiguities behind those syncretic structures can be framed by juxtaposing seemingly inconsistent ways that *mahasiswa* describe Indonesian as they and others use it.

Bahasa Kupang's role as an other-than-standard complement to Indonesian extends to its place in the integrationist dynamic now shaping NTT as a whole. Increased mobility among its speakers now gives this language of urban modernity new kinds of visibility and value beyond the city, causing it to become provincial in a different sense of the word. What might sound marginal and backward outside NTT is now a mode of interethnic communication within the province, with capacities to engender regionally based senses of interactional solidarity. In this way students' verbal engagements with each other can be seen as engagements also with their province and nation at large.

Urban Natives and Newcomers

Cornelis Lay was born in Kupang in 1959 when it was, in his words, "still a very quiet semi-rural provincial town." His parents, as newcomers from the island of Sabu, 150 miles west, acquired the local vernacular they needed for work, in the market, and in their ethnically diverse neighborhood. These were some of the highly variable, nonnative varieties of Malay heard in the town.[2]

Lay, however, acquired Malay natively, with friends, as the language of "nothing less than a *gemeinschaft* with a strong face" (2014: 163). So distinctive were the "games and the languages they created" that Lay's father could

> only understand a bit of what we said. . . . It took him a long time to understand then begin to use some of it. This was the case in most families. . . . Any kid who could not follow our pronunciation, or used one of our words at the wrong time, would be quickly expelled from our circle of play. . . . If anyone asked us what we were talking about, we would spontaneously answer: "If you don't understand, go away."[3] (Lay 2014: 163)

For Lay, unlike his parents and other migrants, the "language of Kupang" was an unethnic mode of engagement with fellow members of age-graded communities of practice.

Lay's parents were early participants in sustained, accelerating patterns of migration which have since caused Kupang to expand rapidly, Now the town's vernacular is spoken natively by some 200,000 residents (Ethnologue 2017) and as a second language by perhaps another 150,000 newcomers.[4]

In 1994, Alo Liliweri concluded from data he gathered using questionnaires that this expansion had not diminished the importance of ethnic difference in everyday life, and in political competition for resources. Ten years later, Thomas Dagang (see Tidey 2012: 13) similarly reported ethnic "closeness" to be an important factor in increasingly stiff competition for entry into the civil service. But Tidey's ethnographic work (2010, 2012, 2014) with members of the political class led her to describe instead conditions of difference and solidarity aligned more with educational background, professional qualifications, and official ranks. These carry over, she observes, to places of residence, choices of lifestyle, patterns of consumption, and so on.

Reports from young persons during our research provide further evidence that ethnic differences are losing some of their salience among Kupang's residents. As Table 2.1 shows, 46 of 90 Kupang natives in this group described themselves as being of "mixed" ethnic background, and 36 of these described Kupang's vernacular, *bahasa Kupang*, as the primary or sole language at home. (Several older persons spoke ruefully to me in interviews about their realization, too late, that their children were coming of age ignorant of "their own" language.) Of 45 newcomers to Kupang, on the other hand, only 8 had parents of different ethnic groups and spoke Kupang's vernacular in their homes.

Table 2.1 Ethnicity and Language Use among Young Educated Kupang Residents

Parents:	# Kupang Natives	# Speaking Kupang Malay Natively	# Kupang Newcomers	# Speaking Kupang Malay Natively
Of different ethnicities	44	36	8	8
Of same ethnicity	46	23	37	10

Young newcomers and natives in Kupang all routinely speak the town's unethnic vernacular, but acquire it at different times in their lives and in different ways. Newcomers encounter it as part of the challenge of city life well after learning standard Indonesian in more rural communities. In those milieux, and particularly in school, they acquire also strong senses of the diglossic regime of standard, and the place of the standard language in national/ethnoregional hierarchies. This can be illustrated with two anecdotes.

Joel Kuipers made the following observation on teacher/student interaction he witnessed in an elementary school in western Sumba, 500 miles west of Kupang:

> When the local language is used, it is employed in a negative context, signaling the fact that the children did not properly understand the question. The use of the local language indicates that the student requires special accommodation on the part of the teacher to help them understand. The students know that they have answered a question incorrectly if the teacher responds by asking the question again in the local language. (1998: 138)

A more extreme incident occurred at a junior high school on the island of Flores when eight students speaking their native Manggarai language before classes were punished with an order to lick the school bathroom. The teacher who forced them to do this was dismissed, the head of the school noted, not because of her purpose but her choice of method (Tribun Wow 2017; Floresa 2017).

Young graduates of high schools outside Kupang find that in the city they need to be able speak as do the great majority of persons they encounter almost everywhere, almost all the time. They learn to do so on the fly, informally, in encounters which are described by my research colleague and longtime Kupang resident, Jermy Balukh, as follows:

> Kupang's vernacular is spoken by everyone in all situations. Uneducated young persons speak it with those who are older and educated, as will a civil servant with an unemployed person, children with parents at home and teachers at school, university students with friends and lecturers, bus drivers with passengers, doctors with patients in the hospital, a high official with his or her staff, or a customer with a market seller.
>
> Students converse in Kupang's vernacular as well as outside their time in class. In elementary school teachers provide explanations in the vernacular, Kupang Malay, so that students do not feel awkward; in secondary schools teachers tend to be more formal and use standard Indonesian to teach, but students consider it to be a language other than their own. Instructions about lessons are given in standard Indonesian, but students discuss them in the vernacular, even when asking questions; they are never reprimanded. The vernacular is actually the primary language of instruction. University students speak the vernacular with each other but also

their lecturers. A lecture in a class must be in Indonesian, but student discussions with each other and lecturers may be in the vernacular regardless of topic. Even a lecturer in the English department uses Kupang Malay to explain or give examples. Students who visit a lecturer's house to discuss an assignment or paper will speak the vernacular (personal communication).

For newcomers, age-mates and peers who are native to Kupang, or who have lived there longer, may offer models for manners of speech they seek to learn. Connections between biography and language competence sometimes surface in interaction between less fluent newcomers and Kupang natives, as Balukh shows:

> Newcomers who mix the vernacular with other [ethnoregional] languages, or speak with the accent of their mother tongue, are considered *orang kampung*, "bumpkins," or *kurang gaul*, "not trendy."[5] Lack of fluency generally makes young people feel inferior to their friends, and over time they seek to reduce the effect of their mother tongues as they become fluent. Young Kupang natives may feel superior to those who do not speak the vernacular fluently. They speak faster, using more contractions (for example, first person singular *bé* rather than *béta* "I," *son* or *on* rather than *sondé* meaning "no, not"). But rate of speech is less important than intonation, accent, and word choice. Newcomers will be accepted as natives if they use the accent that is common among young people (personal communication).

Fluency in Kupang's vernacular is thus acquired and evaluated in the course of interaction and in the absence, as one person pointed out in a 2010 Facebook post (no longer available), of any "standard rule . . . to protest when *bahasa Kupang* is pronounced with different regional accents . . . speakers themselves will try to fit in with their speech partners or environment where they live."[6] Failure may lead to intimate, indirect sanctions, as Balukh demonstrates with a hypothetical scenario in which a fluent speaker of *bahasa Kupang* echoes less fluent use by another:

> when the conversation is in [a] group, especially in informal conversation, then [a newcomer] . . . might [be] ridiculed in case [some]one repeats the [nonfluent] word or phrase the way they do, or they will be asked not to use such [a] word, phrase, or intonation anymore when speaking. For example, [if] a Manggaraian person speaks Kupang Malay in the way s/he speaks Manggarai with [the] particle *ka*, [some]one will repeat it, pronouncing such [a] particle only to remind him/her that it is uncommon in

Kupang.[7] Or pronouncing a word as *bangunan* ['building'] with the stress on the first syllable and long vowel [*a*] on the last syllable is identified as Manggaraian. [This] way of pronouncing *bangunan* could be imitated by someone else as an indirect admonition or even as a joke. Sometimes those speaking fluent Kupang Malay laugh at those who do not when the identified accent or intonation [strongly] indicates a local or vernacular accent. (personal communication)

Such conversational moves are minor ripples in interactional life, but presuppose and teach a durable, shared awareness of what count as expressively authentic registers of urban modernity. They can likewise have momentary but cumulative levelling effects on the ways "the language of Kupang" is spoken without identifiable verbal marks of persons' ethnoregional background.

These dynamics, over time and in the aggregate, contribute to the development of Kupang's vernacular as an urban koiné, that is, a variety of speech that comes into common use among speakers who avoid or strip away structural variants (Siegel 1993). The result is is comparable to other vernaculars of "innovative urban insularity" (Taeldeman 2005: 269), but also to the koiné now known as *bahasa Jakarta* (Wouk 1991).

The Vernacular Base

Empirical evidence of this convergence can be drawn from recordings of everyday talk that was done, mostly among *mahasiswa*, for this research.[8] These help to identify features of what can be called the vernacular base of this koiné listed in Table 2.2.[9] The leftmost column lists cognate and bivalent forms that can be distinguished by provenance as either Kupang Malay or standard Indonesian. Numbers of occasions of use of each are shown in each row for informal conversations, differentiated for the background of persons recorded as *mahasiswa* who were either Kupang natives or newcomers.

Except for the verbs *pigi/pergi*, meaning "go," in the top row, all have grammatical functions (combining with lexical material) or deictic functions ("pointing to" persons, things, and topics presupposed in a context of use). Except for *sondé* and *tidaq* ("no," "not"), similarities of sound shape reflect historical relatedness between forms, including the patterned contrast between monosyllabic Kupang Malay and disyllabic Indonesian cognates (*su* vs. *sudah*, *sa* vs. *saja*, *ju* vs. *juga*, *déng* vs. *déngan*). Kupang Malay *lai* is pronounced without the consonant which opens the second syllable of standard Indonesian *lagi*.[10]

Table 2.2 Frequencies of Use of Common Vernacular and Standard Forms

Vernacular/Standard (Translation)	Kupang Natives # Tokens, % Vernacular	Kupang Newcomers # Tokens, % Vernacular
pi, pigi/pergi (go)	1,312/22, 98	603/18, 97
karmana/bagaimana, gimana* (interrogative)	101/28, 78	134/17, 88
su/sudah (already, finished)	1,948/589, 76	981/236, 80
sa/saja (only, just)	774/84, 90	383/43, 90
son, sondé/tidaq, ndaq** (no)	2,653/226, 92	1,264/119, 91
ju/juga (also)	861/244, 78	515/123, 80
lai/lagi (more, again)	259/132, 66	263/47, 85
déng/déngan (with)	542/305, 64	294/174, 62

* Includes occurrences of *kermana*, another Kupang variant

** Commas separate full and short pronunciations of Indonesian forms; figures represent occurrences of both.

Use of the Malay forms was equally common among newcomers and natives, as was also the case for pronunciations of the cognate trisyllabic forms shown in Table 2.3.

Table 2.3 Pronunciation of Cognate Trisyllabics

Vernacular/ Standard (Translation)	# a/ə Pronunciations, % Vernacular Usage
katawa/kətawa (laugh)	14/30, 41
kapala/kəpala (head)	4/14, 22
tarima/tərima (receive)	21/86, 20
sandiri/səndiri (alone)	51/318, 14
bagitu/bəgitu (like that)	125/1020, 11
bagini/bəgini (like this)	76/688, 9
garéja/gəréja (church)	3/133, 2

The initial vowels of Kupang Malay roots are pronounced rather like the standard American English pronunciation of the first vowel in "father," written here as *a*. In standard Indonesian the corresponding vowel is pronounced more like the second vowel of "sofa," written here as ə, and called schwa. Examples of this contrasting pronunciation, or "accent," are *katawa/kətawa*, "laugh," as in the vernacular talk transcribed as examples 1 and 2. Unlike the Kupang Malay pronunciation in example 1, the standard Indonesian pronunciation in 2 could count as marking a "borrowing" that is combined with vernacular forms *ais* (rather than *habis*), and *bé* (rather than *saya*).

1. Dia han katawa-katawa sa.
   He just laughed and laughed.
2. Ais tu bé ketawa di atas ojèq.
   After that I laughed on the back of the motorcycle.

Broader "preferences" for use of Indonesian lexical material with the vernacular base can be inferred from patterns of pronunciations of the disyllabic cognates shown in Table 2.4. These suggest similarly variable preferences for an Indonesian "accent" among native and newcomer *mahasiswa*.

Table 2.4 Pronunciation of Cognate Disyllabics

Vernacular/Standard (Translation)	Kupang Natives # Tokens, % Vernacular	Kupang Newcomers # Tokens, % Vernacular
tu:tu/tutup (close)	0/25, 0	0/35, 0
i:ka/ikat (tie)	2/7, 22	2/20. 10
pè:ndé/péndéq (short)	1/10, 1	5/34, 13
sa:ki/ sakit (sick)	7/42, 17	14/97, 13
ki:ci/kecil (small)	14/68, 17	46/181, 20
ta:ku/takut (afraid)	9/29, 24	19/59, 24
li:ha/lihat (see)	108/139, 43	191/300, 39
ba:nya/banyaq (many)	82/103, 44	190/280, 40
du:du/duduk (sit)	52/33, 61	80/73, 52
ba:é/baiq (good)	110/44, 70	326/204, 80
da:pa/dapat (find, be able)	147/79, 60	205/149, 58

In Kupang Malay the first vowel, indicated here with a colon, is pronounced with slightly greater stress and length than the second. In Indonesian vowels in cognate roots have similar stress and length. Indonesian roots also end, unlike their Kupang Malay cognates, with a voiceless consonant: *p*, *t*, or glottal stop, transcribed here as *q*. Examples 3 and 4 illustrate this contrast as it occurred in a conversation about acquaintances who were ill:

3. Padahal dia su *saki* bagitu ba lama dua taon katanya.
   But he had been sick so long, two years he said.
4. Dua ana bahasa Inggris yang *sakit* kan di situ to dong tinggal.
   Two English-language students who are sick live there, right?

If Kupang Malay were a "low" ethnoregional language these would count as examples of anomalously "biaccentual" usage. In example 4 the Indonesian pronunciation of the word meaning sick (*sakit*, not *sa:ki*) contrasts directly with that of the word meaning 'child' (*a:na*, not *anaq*). Examples 5–7 illustrate a few "mixed" pronunciations of cognates meaning "many" (see Table 2.4). Italics are used to transcribe forms pronounced as in Kupang Malay; boldface is used to transcribe distinctly Indonesian forms; others are bivalent.

5. Dia *pu ana pung* **banyaq** *lai*.
   She has a lot of children.
6. **Berapa** *ba:nya*?
   How many?
7. *Bé pu* nomor *talalu* **banyaq makanya** *bé* bingung
   I have too many (cell phone) numbers, that's why I'm confused.

These are seemingly minor instances of talk on which the regime of standard Indonesian has little purchase, or is bracketed. But they show how syncretic registers of speech cohere as a vernacular of urban modernity for these students. Such "biaccentual" talk is tacitly enabled by standard Indonesian's unnativeness on one hand, and the unethnic character of the vernacular to which it is assimilated on the other. These linguistic resources are available in the absence of native or "authentic" speakers of either a national or ethnic language.

These syncretic patterns of combination can be considered next as backdrop for use of more interactionally focused personal pronouns and kin terms.

Terms for Persons

In Indonesia, as in much of the world, languages provide means for marking and mediating senses of relation between speakers, persons spoken to (addressees), and those spoken about (so-called third persons) (see, e.g., Enfield and Stivers 2007). In this regard, personal pronouns and kin terms are interactionally or pragmatically salient elements of speech (Errington 1985, 1988) because their conventional referential meanings are bound up with their expressive or intersubjective import in use. They are relatively meaningful as means for presupposing or shifting participants' relations or "alignment[s] to each other and the others present" (Goffman 1981: 128).

To use a Kupang Malay word that can be glossed as "mother" when asking "Where is mother going?" (rather than "Where are you going?") is to mark or presuppose one of two kinds of mutuality between speaker and addressee. Should an adult woman so queried reply using a kin term meaning "child" to identify the questioner, or no kin term at all, an asymmetric pattern of exchange is created, presupposing that she is related to her speech partner as senior to junior, or superior to subordinate. Should she return a term that could be glossed as "father" or "mother," however, a more symmetric pattern of exchange would presuppose that they are of comparable status and age, and perhaps not too familiar with one another. To identify oneself with a kin term in speech to another can have similar expressive import, as when someone says of herself, "Mother is going now" (which can convey analogous senses of intimacy and speakers' seniority).

Data in Table 2.5 demonstrate the almost categorical use of Kupang Malay kin terms among persons we recorded, irrespective of context, and for a wide range of persons other than members of speakers' families.

Table 2.5 Pronunciation of Cognate Kin Terms in Use for Speech Partner

Vernacular/Standard (Translation)	Kupang Natives # Tokens, % Vernacular	Kupang Newcomers # Tokens, % Vernacular
a:na/anaq (child)	245/86, 70	384/163, 70
ka:ka/kakaq (older sibling)	103/2, 95	201/13, 94
ba:pa/bapaq (father)	83/0, 98	202/5, 97

A dispreference for Indonesian terms is especially evident in relatively formal contexts in which the regime of the standard would apply most clearly. Even a minor shift in "accent" when using a kin term can accomplish a shift in alignment between a speaker and someone they are both addressing and identifying. Example 8, for instance, transcribes the beginning of an interview between a researcher and an older, respected male acquaintance. While arranging equipment, the researcher first used the word meaning "father," pronounced as in Indonesian—*bapaq*, with syllables of equal length and final glottal stop—as a vocative, that is, to signal that he should direct attention to the interview that was about to begin. But then she went on to explain the topic using the Kupang Malay pronunciation: "*ba:pa*." A shift in "accent" created a shift in interactional dynamic from her announcement of the beginning of an interactional event to the polite identification of interlocutor and the event's topic: Indonesian politics.

8. *Bapaq*, mo dengar cerita **ba:pa** tèntang prosès dan tahapan pemilihan umum tingkat propinsi sekarang ini.
   Bapaq, I want to hear your (**ba:pa**'s) story about the process and the steps in the general provincial election at present.

Such transitory "switches" between standard and vernacular kin terms can express familiarity or solidarity, whether or not a topic or context of interaction presupposes use of standard Indonesian. A similar shift occurred during a conversation between two *mahasiswa* whose predominant use of standard Indonesian was appropriate for the tone and topic of their discussion. But their familiarity was affirmed by one when he used a vernacular kin term to identify the other.

9. Apalagi khususnya masih di Kupang ini **ka:ka** bolèh omong seperti itu.
   All the more, especially in Kupang you (**ka:ka**) can still talk like that.

Kupang Malay kin terms predominate in conversations we recorded, which illustrate a commonplace way that educated persons engage each other both as fellow urbanites and educated Indonesians.

Personal pronouns, unlike kin terms, serve to identify persons through their relations to acts of speech as speaker, addressee, or others. Instance of use in recordings demonstrate the same preference for vernacular forms, as shown in Table 2.6.

Table 2.6 Occasions of Use of Personal Pronouns

Vernacular/Standard (Gloss)	# Tokens, Vernacular/Standard	% Vernacular
béta, bé/saya* (1st singular)	6,001/337	95
kotong/kita (1st plural inclusive)	1,090/473	70

Table 2.6 continued

Vernacular/Standard (Gloss)	# Tokens, Vernacular/Standard	% Vernacular
botong/kami (1ˢᵗ plural exclusive)	179/36	80
lu/kamu (2ⁿᵈ singular)	1,166/20	98
dorang, dong/ méréka (3ʳᵈ plural singular)	3,292/127	96

Bé is a short form of *béta*. *R*recordings also include 20 tokens of the standard but familiar Indonesian *aku*.

These are common in otherwise standard Indonesian usage, as in example 10, taken from a young man's explanation of his professional credentials. He interspersed his Indonesian with acts of self-reference as *béta,* not standard Indonesian *aku* or *saya.*

10. Bukan ilmu akuntansi yang *béta* terapkan di hidup.
    Accounting's not what *I* do for a living.

While explaining a project being carried out in a government office, another young man made the remark transcribed as example 11, speaking standard Indonesian except for the Kupang Malay pronoun *kotong*, which he used to identify himself and his officemates (not the persons being addressed) rather than Indonesian *kami.*

11. Sebenarnya bukan seperti yang *kotong* buat-buat sekarang.
    Actually it's not like what *we* [inclusive] are doing now.

Slightly more complex was use of the vernacular second-person pronoun *lu* in an otherwise standard Indonesian remark transcribed as example 12. The interviewee mentioned earlier was explaining legal procedures following a contested election, and at this point temporarily shifted his interactional alignment to his interviewer by animating or modeling words a judge might say to a participant in the courtroom. In this guise he spoke standard Indonesian, save for his use of this vernacular second person pronoun rather than the seemingly more appropriate, formal Indonesian *anda* (you) or perhaps a kin term such as *bapak, ibu,* or *saudara.*

12. Hakim putus "oh ini Ka Pé U salah *lu* yang benar" ya silakan.
    (If) the judge decides "Oh, the regulations are wrong, *you*'re right," then
    go ahead.

This is a rare but clear example of the ways that Indonesian and Kupang Malay
figure together in speech, modulating senses of interactional intimacy or solidarity between members of Kupang's political class.

Lexicons of Modernity

More striking patterns of "mixed use" occur when topics of conversation lead to
the syncretization of Indonesian and English lexical material to vernacular registers of speech. These are conspicuous because these lexical items are tied semantically and socially to registers of what Pramoedya called "school language." Yet
speakers routinely incorporate lexical items from national Indonesian and "foreign" English into otherwise vernacular talk. These can be illustrated here with
examples of such lexical material in a distinctly Kupang grammatical constructions for identifying wholes and parts, or possessors and possessions.

13a. Kupang Malay:
     Bé bawa   *bé*   *pung*   *hèlm*   sandiri.
     I bring   I   [POSSESSIVE] helmet   alone/mine.
13b. Standard Indonesian:
     Saya bawa   *hèlm*   *saya*   sendiri.
     I   bring   helmet   I   alone/mine.

     I brought my own helmet.

Example 13a shows how the the Kupang Malay grammatical element *pung*
functions to link preceding and following material as referring to a possessor/
whole (*bé*, I) and a possession/attribute (*hèlm*, helmet) respectively. In standard
Indonesian these constituents combine in the reverse order, the first referring to
possession/attribute (*hèlm*) and the second to possessor/whole (*saya*, I).[11]

In casual speech we recorded *mahasiswa* used constructions with *pung* roughly
3,500 times, over and against fewer than 300 uses of the standard Indonesian construction. Many were nominal constructions formed with distinctly Indonesian
circumfixes. Some, like those in Example Group 2.1A, were formed with *ke—an*,
others with *pel/r—an*, as in group B.

EXAMPLE GROUP 2.1 Vernacular/Standard Possessive
Constructions

A. *Pung* constructions with Indonesian nominals formed with *ke—an*

    penting (important)/*kepentingan* (importance)
        Buat *dong pung kepentingan* parté politik . . .
        For the *needs of their* political party . . .

    mampu (capable of)/*kemampuan* (ability)
        dengan istila-istila dong *pung kemampuan* tèknis untuk atasi itu
        with the terms and *their ability* to overcome that (problem)

    ada (there is)/*keadaan* (the existence of, circumstance)
        Lu bayangkan *lu pung keadaan* karmana misalnya?
        You're imagining *you're in what circumstance* for instance?

B. *Pung* constructions with Indonesian nominals formed with *pe(r/l)—an*

    buat (make, do)/*perbuatan* (action, deed)
        Ia *satu pung perbuatan* samua kena
        yeah, *the deed of one* and everyone took the consequences

    teliti (examine)/*penelitian* (research)
        Bé *pung penelitian* yang *béta* temukan ini . . .
        My research, what I found was this . . .

    ngerti (understand)/*pengertian* (understanding, conception)
        Dong-dong pung pengertian yang baéq yang bagus
        Their understanding is good

Pung serves a related function, comparable with that of the Indonesian suffix *-nya*, as what Englebretson (2003: 161) calls an identifiability marker. Used in this way *-nya* marks the referent of lexical material to which it is suffixed as being identifiable from prior talk and context, rather like the use of a definite article "the" in English. Kupang Malay *pung* functions similarly when combined with the bivalent third-person pronoun *dia*. This comparability can be seen from an occasion when a speaker produced two utterances serially, to reinforce a point, but with different constructions. This man first attached *-nya* to the nominal *persaingan* ('competition,' from the root *saing*) in example 14a to identify his topic in ongoing discussion of an upcoming election. Then he echoed himself, as in 14b, using the Kupang Malay *dia pung* construction.[12]

14a. Tapi ini kan persaingan*nya* aga ketat?
   But this competition is going to be kind of close, right?
14b. Tiga ini *dia pung* persaingan ketat.
   [For] these three the competition is close.

This parallel between Kupang Malay and Indonesian does not extend to uses of Indonesian *-nya* as what Englebretson calls an epistemic marker. This involves a small but frequently used group of roots which *-nya* marks as serving to characterize the evidential basis or perceived relevance of a state of affairs.[13] Uses of Indonesian *-nya* as an epistemic marker occurred about 1,500 times in conversations we recorded, illustrated in examples 15–17 with three of the commonest constructions.

15. Iya dia waktu jato ada hamil itu *kayanya*.
   Yeah when she fell she was pregnant, *it seems*.
16. *Masunya* kotong kaé maso di komputer a?
   It means we have to enter it into the computer?
17. *Pokonya* kalo ada kelebihan dia bagi kasi orang.
   The main thing is if there's extra he'll share it.

These examples show also that although no analogous construction exists in Kupang Malay, this Indonesian grammatical element is regularly syncretized to vernacular pronunciations of roots to which it is suffixed. All these disyllabic were pronounced in the vernacular manner discussed earlier, with longer first syllables and open second syllables: *ka:yanya, ma:sunya,* and *po:konya,* rather than *kayaqnya, maqsudnya,* and *pokoqnya.*[14]

These are just a few of the ways that structural similarities between historically related dialects enable syncretic speech in these communities of practice. They illustrate also the kinds of talk that is tacitly enabled by Indonesian's unnativeness, and in the absence of native speaking examplars in Kupang and beyond.

This same absence can be seen as indirectly facilitating similar assimilations of lexical material of English provenance to vernacular interaction, as illustrated in Example Group 2.2. These are just a few of many uses of conspicuously "foreign" terms we recorded in constructions with *pung,* transcribed in italics. They are likely recognizable to readers with no knowledge of Indonesian save perhaps *strakcèr,* "structure," in example 8.

EXAMPLE GROUP 2.2   English Nouns in Vernacular
Possessive Constructions

---

1. Siswa bikin kesalahan tu dong *pung réaksi* karmana?
   When the students make a mistake what's *their reaction*?
2. ... untuk mewujud nyatakan *méréka pung stratèji* itu.
   ... to shape and make real *their strategy*.
3. Andia to aba mo gambar polisi layang *dia pung posisi* supaya sebentar
   So the friend wanted the police picture *of the position* so that later on ...
4. Na sekarang *dong pung prosès* sampé di mana?
   So how far has *the process* gone?
5. Tanya pengalaman kerja *lu pung rèfèrènsi* su ada.
   [If they] ask about work experience *your references* are ready.
6. Asal usul *dia pung habitat*nya dia dari situ asalnya dari situ.
   The beginning of *its habitat* was from there, its origin was from there.
7. Apa mengerti tiap orang *pung karakter* ni kan béda-béda?
   Do [they] understand each person's *character* is different?
8. *Dia pung strakcèr* karmana lai?
   So what else about *its structure*?
9. Ora kétong pertama musti rubah dong *pung persèpsi é* ...
   First we should change *their perception* ...
10. Dong pung ana ana dong pung *baiodata*
    The children's, the children's *biodata*.

Social and Linguistic Biographies

These data and examples document some of the many ways that talk in Kupang eludes the regime of the standard, and shows that newcomers recognize the value of and seek fluency in Kupang Malay. The ways they gain facility in vernacular fashions of speaking, however, differ from those of their native counterparts. As suggested earlier, biographical differences between newcomers and natives to the city may be evident in competences in standard Indonesian, but also in relative normative senses, stronger or weaker, of the regime that governs its use. Such awareness can be transient, variable, and not directly inferable from habits of speech. So too these subjective orientations are not always open to explicit descriptions, which is why we approached them indirectly with a range of language-related reports and observations. These were provided by young persons during interviews, and serve here an interpretive and contrastive framing of their orientations to a national ideology and local practices.

Most of these one-on-one interviews, of between 20 and 30 minutes, were conducted by younger members of our research team with 30 young educated persons, half Kupang natives and half newcomers. I focus here on their responses to just those queries summarized and tabulated in Table 2.7.

Table 2.7 Responses to Queries

	Native Respondents (8 M, 7 F)*	Newcomer Respondents (7 M, 8 F)*
Reports of competence		
1. # reporting fluency in Indonesian	12 (0.8) (7 M, 5 F)**	15 (1.0) (7 M, 8 F)
2. # reporting fluency in Kupang's vernacular	15 (1.0) (8 M, 7 F)	11 0.7 (4 M, 7 F)**
Report of use		
3. With a teacher on campus	Indonesian: 11 Vernacular: 1	Indonesian: 9 Vernacular: 4
Responses to queries		
4. # affirming the statement "Young people in this town generally speak good Indonesian." ***	12 (0.8) (7 M, 5 F)	5 (0.3) (0 M, 5 F)
5. # answering "Yes" to query: "Have you ever felt awkward speaking Indonesian?"	11 (0.7) (6 M, 5 F)	4 (0.3) (2 M, 2 F)
6. # reporting fluent Indonesian AND answering "yes" to query 5	9 (0.75) (6 M, 3 F)	4 (0.3) (2 M, 2 F)

* Genders of respondents indicated as M = male and F =female.

** Others reported "fair" competence.

*** Responses were elicited with a four-degree scale: agree, disagree, strongly agree, strongly disagree.

The first query, posed in standard Indonesian at the outset of each interview, was: "What languages do you control?" (*Bahasa apa saja yang anda kuasai?*). Interviewees were asked to describe their active and passive competences in both oral and literate language varieties (including digital media). Each mentioned at least two or three languages. Those who did not spontaneously mention English or Jakarta's vernacular were asked about those as well. Their reports on active, oral competences in Indonesian are summarized in row 1.

Then interviewees were asked about their parents and grandparents: their places of birth, residence, ethnic backgrounds, and language competences. Next they were asked to describe the ways they would speak in a series of 40 hypothetical scenarios, briefly described with respect to locales, interlocutors (familial, ethnic, familiar or not), topics, presence of bystanders, and use of media (texting, pop songs, reading, etc.). Row 3 of Table 2.7 summarizes their self-descriptions for just one of these: speaking on a college campus with an instructor. (Interviewees who had not yet begun their college educations did not answer this query.)

Then, in an effort to broaden the conversation, interviewees were asked whether they agreed or disagreed with a series of six statements about Indonesian and other languages. Row 4 of Table 2.7 summarizes their responses to just one: "Young people in this town generally speak good Indonesian." Interviews closed with seven wide-ranging questions which were intended to encourage interviewees to say whatever seemed relevant to them about their and others' language use. Row 5 of Table 2.7 summarizes their responses to one of these: "Have you ever felt awkward speaking Indonesian?" A few narratives elicited with this query are transcribed with English translations in Appendix 2.1.

Initial self-reports of language competences can be seen as partly correlating with the biographies of those who provided them: a few more Kupang natives reported themselves fluent in *bahasa Kupang,* and a few more Kupang newcomers reported themselves fluent in *bahasa Indonésia.* But these self-descriptions need to be considered along responses they provided to the query, reproduced in row 5, as to whether they had ever felt awkward speaking Indonesian. 9 of the 12 Kupang natives who initially described their Indonesian as fluent also described encounters in which they felt dysfluent: job interviews, interaction with people from outside NTT, when giving formal presentations in class, and so on. Only 4 of 11 newcomers who reported themselves fluent in Indonesian provided similar narratives.

On the face of things these responses appear inconsistent and so perhaps unreliable. But they can be interpreted instead as complementary, as are the queries which elicited them. A relative weaker orientation to the regime of the standard among Kupang natives might be reflected in self-evaluations that keyed less to fluency in a language's structures than to facility in a language of urban more than national modernity. This resonates with Balukh's description of the ways they acquired standard Indonesian forms, and conduct themselves as educated persons. In this context, having easy recourse to Indonesian lexicons of modernity could be a more salient as a mark of fluency than use of the vernacular base sketched earlier.

Newcomers who acquired Indonesian in more literacy-centered and regimented contexts, on the other hand, might have responded with a stronger orientation to the regime of the literate standard, which they acquired before they came to the city. That same prescriptive stance might be inferred from the relatively greater number of critical evaluations by newcomers of Indonesian as spoken by their Kupang age-mates, summarized in row 4 of Table 2.7.

A similar contrast can be drawn from students' self-descriptions of their talk with teachers on a university campus, summarized in row 3. Of 11 Kupang natives who reported using Indonesian in such situations, 8 later reported experiences of dysfluency when speaking that language. On the other hand, all 4 newcomers who reported speaking Kupang's vernacular (*bahasa Kupang*) in that context had previously reported their competences in that language to be only fair.

These partial inconsistencies might reflect concrete differences in Indonesian competence, or different senses of its distinctness from vernacular registers of speech. A weaker orientation to the regime of the standard may have led some natives to orient their response less to properties of speech than the context in question: how else would one speak to a teacher, on campus, but in Indonesian? When recollecting particular interactional experiences, on the other hand, they describe events in which they felt themselves to be in less than full conformance with the regime of the standard. Newcomers with a stronger orientation to the distinctive features of standard Indonesian, on the other hand, could report themselves as speaking Kupang's vernacular to a teacher because such use, fluent or not, was relatively more appropriate.

Though these interviews were relatively few in number, and conducted with members of a fairly homogeneous group, they help at least identify multiple and shifting perceptions of differences between what Pramoedya called "working language" and "school language." When responses are decontextualized they provide a somewhat artificial illustration of variable senses of Indonesian speakership among members of an urban community and a national citizenry. This variability, like the kinds of talk students evaluated for us, is enabled by the absence of native speakers of "the best Indonesian."

The Intimacy of Mixed Messages

These other-than-standard Indonesians are not structurally interstitial ("mixed") but expressively coherent registers (or linguistic figurings) of membership in communities of practice. They derive value from the place they are spoken, a locus of urban "modernity" and "blind spot" for the regime of the standard. The use of the town's vernacular among these more educated residents extends to use of lexical material not just from standard Indonesian but English as another "virtual resource," to borrow Widdowson's observation on International English, that can be "variously actualized" for "changing needs" (1997: 142).

In some contexts the relevance of the regime of the standard can become visibly contested. One such event became a topic of conversation that happened to be recorded between three female *mahasiswa*—Ina, Lina, and Rina. They were chatting in a room shared by two of them when talk turned to plans for the upcoming weekend. Ina said that she had been called by her mother to go home to the nearby island of Alor (Transcript 2.1).

Transcript 2.1 Going Home to Alor

I: Saturday I'm going home.	I: Hari Saptu bé su pulang.
L: Going home to Alor? Don't go, I'll be alone here.	L: Su pulang Alor? Ado jang dolu pulang ko, nanti kita sendiri saja di sini ni.
I: I'm going. Last night Mama phoned, told me to come home.	I: Pulang la. Tadi malam Mama tua dong tèlpon suruh pulang.
L: When I go back to Alor, it means when I'm on ship, when I get off, the boat anchors in the harbor, I get off I have to flick my tongue . . .	L: Oh pulang Alor berarti harus sampé di kapal. Pas mau turun ini, pas kapal sandar di pelabuhan tu, turun harus kuti lida ooo
I: What for?	I: O supaya apa?
L: So I don't use "*béta sondé*," no "*sondé.*" When I get to Alor it has to be "*saya.*" "*Saya* am going to the market, *Saya* am going shopping."	L: Supaya jang omong logat "béta sondé" ko sondé éé ko tida. Sampé di Alor tu harus "saya." "Saya mau pi pasar, saya mau pi belanja."
I: Well using "*pi*" [go] is all right.	I: Mau "pi" ju tida apa-apa ya.
L: . . . no, you can't, later you just let it sneak in . . . sometimes they tell me, the first time, one time "don't bring that *sondé* of yours here, we don't need *sondé* here, no."	L: . . . tida nanti terahir omong su kecolongan bahasa . . . kadang-kadang bilang ini pertama satu kali "sondé ma, hmm pikol-pikol lu pung sondé datang sini, orang sondé butuh lu pung sondé di sini tidak."
R: In Kéfa folks are like that too. "Saya, tidak."	R: Orang Kéfa dong ju begitu. "Saya, tidak."

Lina, from a different part of Alor, protested against being left alone, and then Ina described what she knew would happen when the ship docked there. She would flick her tongue with a finger to remind herself not to speak *bahasa*

Kupang, but would not entirely avoid urban habits of speech she had acquired. This would draw criticism from folks back home, and instructions to avoid using vernacular words like *béta* ("I, me," standard Indonesian *saya*) and *sondé* ("no, not," standard Indonesian *tidak*). Rina echoed her prediction sympathetically, alluding to similar experiences in her hometown of Kéfa, in the Timorese highlands.

Ina presented an ironic, double-voiced version of this encounter, partly narrating and partly performing what she foresaw would happen. Rather than describing what would be said by folks back home to her ("They say to me . . .") she imitated or modeled their utterances, presupposing that Lina and Rina would recognize that she was momentarily switching her interactional alignment to them from addressees to audience for her performance. But to perform what folks "back home" said she put in their mouths same words they criticized her for using (italicized here): "pikol-pikol *lu pung sondé* datang sini, orang *sondé* butuh *lu pung sondé* di sini tidak" [don't bring that *sondé* of yours here, we *don't* need *your sondé* here, no].[15]

This brief performance might be evidence of how thoroughly Ina had assimilated urban habits of speech. But it also enacted, with and for her friends, a sense of connection-and-difference with absent others "back home." It invited (and got) empathetic responses from friends with similar biographies and experiences.

This passing narration/performance fits well Michael Herzfeld's (1997) broader account of conduct that can engender intimacy among persons through a shared sense of "external embarrassment" relative to absent persons. In this event individuals shared and supported an interactional demeanor (a manner of speaking) at the same time that they shared an awareness of the ways it deviates from dominant norms (here, the regime of the standard). Rina and Lina could recognize and appreciate Ina's enactment of talk "back home" because they also speak in ways that incorporate "inward flaws and imperfections" to which dominant norms are "officially and ostensibly opposed" (1997: 172). They too understood her feeling of "external embarrassment" in such encounters with folks "back home," and perhaps with other speakers of "good Indonesian" in the nation at large.

What Herzfeld calls an "assurance of common sociality" (1997: 3) can emerge in conduct which incorporates an ambient awareness of absent, more or less anonymous others. This awareness is underwritten, in the case of Indonesian, by the diglossic regime of the standard. This is a linguistic instance of what Herzfeld identifies more broadly as "disemia," which I discuss in Chapter 4 relative to practices and symbols that legitimize dominant segments of national societies (1997: 14). In this context, however, dominant norms of

Indonesian are tied to institutions of the state rather some native-speaking part of the nation.

Syncretic use of lexicons of modernity, on the other hand, might generate intimacy through a different way of flouting the regime of the standard. Consider this exchange, drawn from a longer, fairly desultory conversation between two friends, Miriam (M) and our researcher Hallie (H) (Transcript 2.2).

Transcript 2.2 Looking for a Dictionary

M: because I don't have a dictionary of agriculture, the technical terms are different, right?	M: karena béta sondé punya kamus pertanian, kan dia pung istila-istila tèknis kan béda.
H: hm, the terminology	H: mm dia pung terminolojis
M: like ... ha the terminology is different, yeah, not like ...	M: macam kaya pem ... haa terminilojisnya béda to bukan yang ...

Miriam, a high school teacher, had asked Hallie for help finding a specialized Indonesian-English dictionary she needed for a translation assignment. She shifted from vernacular (*béta sondé* "I don't") to a standard Indonesian phrase (*punya kamus pertanian*), followed by a vernacular *dia pung* construction with the word *istila* (of Indonesian provenance, but pronounced in a vernacular manner without the final *h*). Hallie responded with *dia pung* as an identifiability marker for English *terminolojis*, which Miriam echoed with Indonesian *-nya* in the same function.

Such exchanges of syncretic speech, fairly common among educated urban intimates, can be about topics which presuppose membership in that small group of Kupang residents whose language competences include English. Easy recourse to national Indonesian and global English (like *terminolojis*) in casual, vernacular registers of speech can in this way presuppose intimacy between them relative to others in the city, and in the nation at large.

Between the Urban and Provincial

Such talk would be regarded by educated Indonesians elsewhere as distinctly marginal and provincial: besides being structurally "mixed" it has distinctive rhythms and intonations that would sound out of place almost anywhere else in the country. Its widespread use might seem to outsiders to be evidence that Kupang is one place where the Indonesian miracle has not yet taken hold fully.

Unequal distribution of competences in standard Indonesian might likewise be seen as a means for reproducing social stratification among Kupang's city's residents, including its political class. Facility in standard Indonesian can distinguish higher levels of professionalism, like that of the office head who required subordinates' written work to be submitted to him for inspection before being sent elsewhere. It can align also with mobility, tied to the economic advantage of persons with means to send their children to Den Pasar on Bali, or Surabaya on Java, to acquire more standard-sounding habits of speech.

But within NTT "the language of Kupang" appears differently. The leveling out of transfer effects from ethnoregional languages attests to a broad orientation to urban commonality, broadly similar to that of the unethnic vernacular of Jakarta. At the same time, *bahasa Kupang* is becoming more widely known in other parts and communities of NTT, and so becoming "provincial" in another sense of the word. Kupang's vernacular can now travel thanks to the same infrastructures of mobility that have enabled the rapidly expanding newcomer presence in the city.

Persons moving between the city and regions, like Ina and her friends, can become vectors for an integrative dynamic within NTT. Whether or not some criticize them "back home" for "bad" habits of speech they picked up in the city, newcomers can then become intimate exemplars of new ways of talking—sophisticated but not standard—connecting peripheries to the city.

Elsewhere in Indonesia such conditions of mobility have given rise to what I discuss in Chapter 4 as regional lingua francas (Zein 2020: 34). More important here is *bahasa Kupang*'s potential value as standard Indonesian's informal, unethnic complement, and an emblem of commonality within one province. Such a sense of provincial solidarity might be invoked among readers of an advertisement posted for NTT's regional development bank on the wall of the departure lounge of Kupang's El Tari Airport. Through this room pass those members of NTT's political class, with resources, interests, and language competences that enable broader engagements with the nation (particularly Jakarta). Members of this well-off, educated demographic are good targets for an advertisement soliciting deposits. That sign appeals to them not in the "good and true" language of national citizenship, but in the vernacular of Kupang and, implicitly, the province. The original wording of the sign appears in the leftmost column in Transcript 2.3.

Transcript 2.3 A Bank Advertisement

Kupang Vernacular	Standard Indonesian	Translation
Jang tunggu lai!	Jangan tunggu lagi!	Don't wait any longer!
Sakarang su, datang ko tabung di	Sekaranglah dating tabung di	Come now to make a deposit at
Tabungan SIMPEDA bank NTT	Tabungan SIMPEDA bank NTT	The NTT Bank regional deposit program

This sign is an example of what Zane Goebel and colleagues (2017) have called the "latent linguistic enfranchisement" of nonstandard and regional languages, which began after the fall of the New Order. But this appeal, made at a threshold between province and nation, invites senses of commonality among persons who share the language of nation but also of a provincial center of urban modernity.

Notes

1. Residents of NTT acknowledge the province's marginality through the popular Indonesian practice of reading acronyms against the grain, as comments on what they name. As Sylvia Tidey notes (2012: 3), two such popular reinterpretations of NTT in Kupang are Nanti Tuhan Tolong (God Will Help Eventually) and Nasib Tak Tentu (Uncertain Future).

2. Liliweri (1994: 3–4) cites a 1981/1982 report by the Center for the Study of History and Culture (Pusat Penelitian Sejarah dan Budaya Pendidikan dan Kebudayaan) distinguishing 15 major ethnic groups (*kelompok utama etnik*), 75 linguistically distinct ethnicities (*kesatuan etnik*), and some 500 subethnic (*subetnik*) or tribal groups.

3. "Wé bosong omong apa tu?/Kalo sondé mangarti pi jao-jao" (translation in the original).

4. In 1977, two years after the New Order invaded Timor Leste, James Fox noted that Kupang was beginning to attract new residents. By the turn of the century it was home to 335 state institutions, forming an "overwhelming physical presence" in the city (Tidey 2012: 28). A population of 80,000 in 1980 had become, by official reports, 300,000 in 2010, though others put the population of the city and its surrounds at 500,000 (*Pos Kupang*, April 26, 1999, cited in Tule 2000). An overview of Kupang's history is provided by Leirissa et al. (1983).

5. Young people make use of a range of expressions that count for them as distinctive of *bahasa gaul*, touched on in Chapters 1 and 4. These differ not only from *bahasa gaul* in Jakarta and other Indonesian cities, but also from group to group and

campus to campus within Kupang itself. The focus here is on forms more widely characteristic of vernacular use.

6. "Yang patut dibanggakan adalah tidak ada suatu aturan baku untuk memprotès ketika bahasa Kupang dilafalkan dengan aksèn daérah masing-masing. Malah penutur itu sendiri akan berusaha menyesuaikan diri dengan lawan bicara atau lingkungan di mana ia tinggal."

7. *Ka* marks the truth or salience of a preceding expression. For instance in response to the question, "Does the top scorer get an award?," a speaker replies, "Dapat ka pasti." This can be translated colloquially as 'Of course,' word by word as "GET" *ka* "CERTAINLY."

8. These and other data in this chapter are drawn from 40 recordings of 26 hours of informal conversation; 74 of the 97 participants in those conversations were younger than 35, and 49 were younger than 22.

9. Descriptions of some of these forms are provided in Grimes and Jacob (2008) and Jacob (2014).

10. A similar contrast, not tabulated here, exists for pronunciations of a preposition meaning "to," pronounced much more often in Kupang as vernacular *ké* rather than standard Indonesian *kə*. Thanks to David Gil for pointing out this obvious and widespread preference. See Rafael (2019) for a broader description of phonological interference in Indonesian among speakers of *bahasa Kupang*.

11. *Pung* also serves as a verb meaning "own, possess," cognate with the standard Indonesian *punya*. So the example below can be translated into Indonesian and English in two different ways, with "*pung*" as a verb (example A) or a possessive marker (example B).

Kupang Malay: Dia   pung   pandangan   lain.
A. Indonesian: Dia   punya   pandangan   lain.
   English: "S/he has a different view."
B. Indonesian: Pandangan—*nya*   lain.
   English: "Their view   differs"

12. *Dia pung* was used as an identifiability marker and topicalizer about 90 times by persons we recorded, as compared with 150 analogous uses of Indonesian *-nya*. These overlapping functions can be seen from the following examples, translatable as "The running of the ball" or "The ball's speed was amazing."

Kupang Malay: Itu   bola   pung   lari   ada   ngeri.
              THAT   BALL   RUN   INTENSIFIER   TERRIFYING.
Indonesian: Lari-   -nya   bola   itu   ngeri.
              RUN   BALL THAT AMAZING.

13. Foong Ha Yap (2011) describes *-nya,* along with other Malay grammatical elements, as an adverbial indicator of evidentiality and stance. Grangé (2015) discusses *-nya*'s function as a deverbal nominalizer indicating perfect aspect; I can find no analogous uses of constructions with *pung* in our data.

14. Vernacular *ka:ya* (102) is much more common in our recordings than standard *kayaq* (36); vernacular *po:ko* (158) slightly more common than standard *pokoq* (123). Standard *maqsud*, on the contrary, is much more common (180 times) than vernacular *maksu* or *masu* (22 times).

15. *Pikol* refers to the act of carrying things, usually heavy, on both ends of a pole over the shoulder. *Pikol-pikol* identifies such actions as repetitive or unnecessary.

3 IDENTIFYING WITH INDONESIAN

Pontianak, like Kupang, became more populous, more heterogeneous, and more closely integrated with its province under the aegis of the New Order. Much more than Kupang, however, it became a site of heightened tension between different ethnic segments of its 640,000 residents. I discuss these conditions first as context for a sketch of Indonesian as a language that some in Pontianak speak in ways that can efface, but not entirely not erase, linguistic marks of ethnic background. These vernacular manners of speaking are sketched for *mahasiswa* of three different ethnic backgrounds. Some are members of Pontianak's centuries-old ethnic Chinese community, long sociopolitically marginal in the nation at large because they having no native ethnoregion. Ethnic Malays, on the other hand, count as native to the city, its immediate surround, and other coastal regions of Borneo. A smaller group of Dayaks are members of West Kalimantan's largest, heavily exploited ethnic group.

Young persons of these and other ethnic backgrounds are among 37,000 *mahasiswa* who attend Pontianak's 25 tertiary educational institutions, all but two established after 1998 (Minza 2012: 74).[1] They have similar educational backgrounds and competences in Indonesian, but nonetheless speak in ways that vary as do their ethnic backgrounds and biographies. The Chinese I discuss here are generally observant of the regime of standard Indonesian, unlike ethnic Malays who commonly and freely assimilate standard Indonesian forms to their native habits of speech. Dayaks, like other newcomers and migrants to Pontianak, and their counterparts in Kupang, acquire other-than-standard varieties of Indonesian they identify not as Malay but the language of the city, *bahasa Pontianak*. I describe these as registers of speech that incorporate elements of Malay but differ from those spoken by Malays, called *bahasa Melayu Pontianak*.

A few data and transcripts help differentiate between these manners of speaking, and unnative Indonesian's roles in this ethnically diverse urban scene. They need to be presented in the context of a

Other Indonesians. Joseph Errington, Oxford University Press. © Oxford University Press 2022.
DOI: 10.1093/oso/9780197563670.003.0003

broad sketch of political and economic conditions that have continually differentiated these three segments of Pontianak's citizenry.

Ethnopolitical Dynamics and Urban Differences

Pontianak's location, at the confluence of the Kapuas and Landak rivers, makes it a key point of transit between Western Borneo's interior and the wider world. The Dutch recognized its logistic value and induced its founder and ruler, Syarif Abdurrahman Alkadrie, to accept their military support in 1779 in return for permission to establish a Chinese enclave there. Under Dutch oversight and protection, speakers of Tio Ciu came to Pontianak primarily to manage mercantile affairs, and soon outnumbered the settlement's ethnic Malay residents.[2] The importance of their economic roles was counterbalanced by their social and political marginality as Chinese "foreigners." They were not native to any region of what was to become the Dutch empire, and stood apart from the "native" colonial subjects called *inlanders* in Dutch, and *pribumi* in Malay and Indonesian. This persistent racial distinction runs through Indonesian history, most obviously and bloodily when Chinese, especially in Indonesian towns, have become political scapegoats and targets of mob violence.

Malays, distinguished by adherence to Islam and fealty to the sultan, served as political surrogates for the Netherlands East Indies. As literate monotheists they counted as more civilized than natives of Borneo's interior, identified by outsiders simply as upriver "Dayaks." Dayaks were regarded as uniformly pagan, primitive, and fit only to serve as vassals to coastal sultans. In fact they lived in diverse locales, spoke different languages, and had different cultures.

An imperial economy, and later the New Order's development agenda, caused Dayaks to be increasingly encroached on by outsiders. In the late nineteenth century, responding to global demand for rubber, colonial agents required Dayaks to harvest rubber on their native lands. Over the next century they were coerced into laboring on rubber plantations on land that was expropriated from them by the Indonesian government (Dove 2011). Massive, largely illegal logging projects soon opened vast swaths of the interior for palm oil plantations, where Dayaks were forced to "labor . . . on their own land. . . . [E]nvironmental destruction has eroded the social life of traditional Dayak communities. Uncounted conflicts large and small [have arisen] between the people and companies, and even among themselves" (Bamba 2008: 21).[3]

An unintended consequence of this sustained exploitative dynamic was the transformation of "Dayak" from an outsiders' term of "contempt and subjugation" into the "charged [and] politicized" name (Davidson 2008: 111) of a newly mobi-lized constituency. The beginnings of this shift can be traced to encounters among young persons who came to Pontianak from West Kalimantan's interior to study at middle and high schools established in the early 1980s.[4] Although they were native speakers of different "Dayak" languages, their educations enabled them to make Indonesian the language of their "budding self-empowerment movement" (Davidson 2008: 228).

Because Indonesian was a language that they shared with educated members of other indigenist movements elsewhere in the country, it enabled the formula-tion of a translocal agenda with national and international visibility. More locally, Indonesian's written forms offered an orthographic model for spoken Dayak lan-guages, and thus the potential for print-literate parity with other ethnoregional languages. Most important here is a local ideological consequence of the regime of the standard: it foreclosed on any claim of linguistic or cultural privilege that might otherwise have been made on behalf of ethnic Malays as native speakers of the ethnoregional language that is "closest," historically and structurally, to that of the nation.[5]

Other New Order actions also indirectly drove "interest in ethnic unity among Christianized Dayaks" (Kartinnen 2005: 276–277). To deal with pop-ulation pressure elsewhere in Indonesia (especially Madura, off Java's northeast coast), the New Order brought transmigrants to what were regarded as "unset-tled" regions of West Kalimantan. By the mid-1990s tensions between transmi-grant and Dayak communities gave way to sporadic but widespread violence, which accelerated after the New Order's fall in 1998. Many transmigrants to West Kalimantan and their descendants were driven from those rural regions and became residents of the province's cities, including Pontianak.[6]

As political control decentralized, open elections ushered in a new dispen-sation, and coalitions of Dayaks and Chinese began to make inroads into the provincial government. So too ethnic tensions heightened to the extent that West Kalimantan's governor deemed data from the 2000 census on Pontianak's ethnic makeup too sensitive to be published; in 2008 the election of a Dayak governor and Chinese vice-governor confirmed a fundamental shift in provincial ethnopolitics, marked also by sporadic clashes between Malays and Chinese in Pontianak itself (Benny Subianto 2009; Nyarwi Ahmad 2008).

Collateral census data led one study group to estimate that in 2000 about 26 percent of Pontianak's residents were Malay, and some 31 percent were ethnic Chinese (Caireu Team 2008). Some of these were members of the Tio Ciu com-munity mentioned earlier; others had ancestors who had migrated to parts of West Kalimantan's interior in the eighteenth century. Soon after the New Order took power these speakers of Khek became targets of suspicion as sympathizers with communists on the Malaysian side of the border. Agents of the new regime instigated Dayaks living in the region to drive Kheks from their settlements (Yuan 2000; Hui 2011). Some now live in regions around Pontianak, many in a neighborhood facing that of Tio Ciu residents across the Kapuas River.

In 2000 Dayaks living in Pontianak were estimated to make up less than 8 percent of the capital's population, but represent there—and in offices of the provincial government—what is now West Kalimantan's single largest ethnic constituency. According to the 2010 census (Na'im and Syaputra. 2010) 2.2 million Dayaks comprise not quite half of West Kalimantan's entire population.[7]

This devolution of political control from Jakarta also led to new public representations of West Kalimantan society as supported by "three pillars" (*tiga tiang*) of ethnicity: Chinese, Malay, and Dayak (see Chan 2009: 134).[8] This image of parity also tacitly accorded primacy to these three groups relative to thousands of migrants and their descendants from other parts of Indonesia, who now comprise some 20 percent of Pontianak's population. The largest such constituency consists of some 70,000 ethnic Buginese whose homeland is in southern Sulawesi, east of Borneo.

Religious differences likewise have new saliences in this expanding, diversifying population. Pontianak's 300,000 Muslims—Malays, Javanese, Madurese, Buginese, and others—now form a constituency distinct from pork-eating Confucians (Chinese) and Christians (Chinese and Dayak). Interethnic solidarity among Muslims can be inferred from the parentage of Muslim participants in our research: 13 of 34 had one Malay and one migrant (but Muslim) parent.[9]

This simple overview of conflict and integrative dynamics in Pontianak, quite different from those in Kupang, provides context for a linguistic sketch of the kinds of Indonesian spoken in this provincial center. It links different varieties, and elements of Indonesian and Malay they syncretize, to their roles as interactional mediators of ethnic difference.

Indonesian and Ethnic Malay Accents

Standard Indonesian and varieties of Malay spoken natively in Pontianak are similar enough that I can focus here on three specific contrasts in "accent," that is, manners of sound production that are diacritic of the provenance of spoken forms. Two are illustrated by Transcript 3.1, drawn from a conversation of about 10 minutes between Alan, a Pontianak native and speaker of Tio Ciu, and Bambang, a Malay newcomer to the city.[10] Their manners of speech were asymmetric in that Alan continually used standard Indonesian while Bambang adopted Malay pronunciations.

Transcript 3.1 Alan and Bambang Chat

Bambang: Nah, kaloq misal*ny*ə pulang malam énté beγani sendiγi sini?

So for instance, are you brave enough to come home at night by yourself?

Alan: Sebenar*nya* ndaq berani sih, hanya nékat aja kaloq maoq pulang malam.

It's not that I'm brave, I just go for it coming home at night.

The commonest accent difference, discussed in some detail later, is between pronunciations of central vowels at ends of words and word roots. In Malay they are pronounced as schwa (written ə), as when Bambang said misal*ny*ə (using the epistemic suffix discussed in Chapter 2). In Indonesian they are pronounced more like the first vowel in a standard American English pronunciation of "father," as when Alan said sebenar*nya* ("actually").

This difference is structurally superficial compared with lexical and grammatical features that distinguish "dialects" or entirely different "languages." But under the regime of the standard it distinguishes a national from an ethnoregional language. Sensitivity to this small but ubiquitous matter of accent was evident in one Malay woman's answer to a query as to whether she ever felt awkward speaking Indonesian:

Yes, when speaking with people who are—from Jakarta and the like, then I (we) get confused. My way of talking isn't fluent, not fluent like people usually. . . . My language, my way of speaking is *"mo ke man*ə*?"* [Malay, "Where are you going?," a typical greeting.] Ah, I forgot, *"mo ke man*ə*?,"* they won't understand, right? *"Ko mo ke man*ə*?"* So (if) I use good Indonesian they'd understand, but I have to think first, oh how is it in good Indonesian so this person understands? Speak incorrectly and people think you're crazy, "This person is crazy." If people don't understand even a little you get called crazy.[11]

Her example, a greeting which is as commonly used when speaking Indonesian as Malay, illustrated different pronunciations of the last vowel of the interrogative marker: *mana* in Indonesian, *man*ə in Malay. She described the latter pronunciation, addressed to the wrong person, as being unintelligible ("They won't understand, right?") or a possible sign of speaker's mental condition ("people think you're crazy.") In the context of an interview this remark may have been a hyperbolic expression of her awareness of the regime of the standard, but it demonstrates the potential relevance of a routine, minor point of variation in speech. It demonstrates also the possible social saliences of speech that might be called "biaccentual," another term that is awkward but useful here for describing syncretic registers of speech that incorporate both pronunciations.

Bambang's other distinctly Malay pronunciation occurred when he said *beɣani* ("brave, willing") and *sendiɣi* ("by oneself") with a consonant I write here as ɣ. This represents a voiced velar fricative, produced with the tongue positioned approximately as when pronouncing *g* in English, but with a narrow opening in the oral cavity. It contrasted with Alan's pronunciation of the first of these words when he responded to Bambang's query, in standard Indonesian, saying the first with a sound transcribed here as *r*, and produced by briefly touching the tip of his tongue to the ridge of the mouth behind the top teeth.

Whether or not Bambang and Alan felt awkward exchanging different "accents," neither adopted a demeanor more like the other's. Their chat is useful for illustrative purposes, but demonstrates patterns of usage that were infrequent in recordings done for this project. More commonly persons interacting across lines of ethnic difference adjusted or *adequated* their verbal demeanors. *Adequation*, a term introduced by Bucholtz and Hall, helps here to describe the ways persons adopt manners of speaking (including "accents") sufficiently "similar for current interactional purposes" (2005: 599).

Another example shows how the interactional salience of asymmetric exchanges can vary with speakers' biographies, and from context to context. Transcript 3.2 is drawn from a chat on a college campus between two Chinese friends. Yuli, a native speaker of Khek, is fluent in Indonesian but adopted a more relaxed way of speaking with her friend Wati. Wati, a native speaker of Tio Chu, has competence in standard Indonesian but not the informal variety used by Yuli.[12] So when conversation turned to the visibility on campus of a mutual acquaintance, Wati echoed Yuli's comment with a different "accent."

Transcript 3.2 Yuli and Wati Chat

Yuli: He-eh, diə pangkatnyə besaq ke.	Yeah, he's got a high rank.
Wati: He-eh, dia pangkatnya besar.	Yeah, he's got a high rank.

Pronunciations of final central vowels as *a* and schwa occurred when they used the indefinite pronoun (*diə* by Yuli, *dia* by Wati), and attached the associative suffix to the root *pangkat* (*pangkatnyə* and *pangkatnya*, respectively).

The third accent difference of interest here occurred when Yuli pronounced a word meaning "large" or "high" in what otherwise could be identified as a Malay manner, with a final glottal stop (*besaq*), whereas Wati pronounced it with standard Indonesian *r* (*besar*).

Yuli's utterance is a first example of vernacular registers of speech that incorporate what count, by provenance, as elements of ethnoregional Malay. Transcript 3.2, compared with Transcript 3.1, also shows how the expressive significances of use of structurally "mixed" forms are interactionally situated, here relative to language competences of participants and the biography of their relationship. Similarly asymmetric patterns of exchange can be seen in this way to mediate different kinds of interactional relations: some across durable lines of ethnic difference, others in relations of familiarity and solidarity.

"Biaccentual" Forms and Syncretic Talk

Together, these three accent contrasts can distinguish talk in either a national or an ethnoregional language. But they figure also in other registers of speech with interactional meanings that vary with speakers' repertoires and interactional dynamics. These can be sketched by showing how features of native Malay figured in syncretic registers of urban speech recorded during our research among persons of various backgrounds.

Slippage between these categories is very clear, for instance, in talk among Malay *mahasiswa* who used both "accents" in a single utterance, like those transcribed in Example Group 3.1.

EXAMPLE GROUP 3.1   Provenance/Style Contrasts:
Word Final schwa and *saja*

---

a. Kan bisə saja dalam waktu tertentu bisə berubah.
   So [it] certainly can, in a certain amount of time, [it] can change.

b. Jadi dari, liat, dari namənya saja kan Tarbiyah?
   So looking just at its name, [it's] Tarbiyah right?

The remark transcribed as 1a includes the Indonesian modifier *saja* ("only, just") and a verb pronounced as in Malay: *bisə* ("be able to"). Later this speaker's interlocutor again used Indonesian *saja* to modify a word pronounced with final schwa in the root (*namə*), and then the associative suffix: *namənya* ("its name"). Such "mixed use" is as widespread among ethnic Malays as among persons other ethnic backgrounds because very few people we recorded ever used the Malay cognate of *saja*, likewise pronounced with final schwa (*sajɔ*). This broad preference is evident from a tabulation of total occasions of use of both in our recordings in Table 3.1.

Table 3.1 Provenance/Style Complementarities

Language: Indonesian (# uses)	Malay (# uses)
Style:	
Formal register	*saja* (56)	*sajɔ* (7)
Casual register	*aja* (99)	*jaq/yaq* (1877)

These disyllabic words have the shorter pronunciations, labeled "casual", in the second row. The first consonant of Indonesian *saja* can be elided, as Alan did in his remark discussed earlier, as a relatively rare mark of informality. In Malay the "short form" is a monosyllable pronounced with a closing glottal stop: *jaq* or *yaq*. Table 3.1 shows an almost categorical preference among speakers we recorded for informal Malay pronunciations on one hand, and more formal Indonesian *saja* on the other.

This provides a clear first example of contrasts between speech elements keying nor ro provenance (Indonesian vs. Malay) but verbal demeanor ("informal" and "formal" registers of speech). Similar but less categorical patterns of slippage can be read from data of use for two other less frequently used modifiers which are tabulated in Appendices 3.1 and 3.2. (The presentation of those data is explained in the discussion of Tables 3.2–3.4 below.)

Dayaks used informal "Malay" *jaq* far more commonly than Indonesian *aja* in otherwise Indonesian speech, and so blurred this contrast between provenance and style.[13] Examples in Group 3.2 show how Dayak students used *jaq* to modify words they pronounced as in Indonesian: *nanya* (vs. *Malay nanyɔ*; "ask") in 2a, and *nama* (vs. Malay *namɔ*; "name") in 2b.

EXAMPLE GROUP 3.2   Provenance/Style Contrasts:
Word Final *a* and jaq

---

a. Ndaq, nany*a* jaq.
No, [he] just asked.

b. Nam*a* jaq udah sekolah Bayangkari.
Its name is the Bayangkari school.

Under the regime of the standard such talk may count as anomalously biaccentual, but it is commonplace in everyday urban life and syncretic conversation. Adoption of these urban manners of speaking allows Dayaks to "sound like" urban habitués, but not like ethnic Malays. In this way they respond to a challenge indirectly identified by one young Dayak in conversation with some others when he described his amusement at another Dayak acquaintance's efforts to acclimatize linguistically.

Transcript 3.3 "I almost die laughing"

Aku setengah mati tekakaqkikiq dengar dia ngomong, maksa diriq pakai bahasa Pontianak, gituq tu.

I almost die laughing when I hear him talk, forcing himself to use Pontianak language.

He described the manner of speech his friend was trying to use as *bahasa Pontianak*, a label like those commonly used for the urban vernaculars of Kupang and Jakarta (*bahasa Kupang, bahasa Jakarta*). In this way he also tacitly identified registers of speech distinct from those associated with ethnic Malays, who for him and other Dayaks count as members of an ethnic outgroup. Perhaps his laughter stemmed from rueful recollection of his own negotiation of this sociolinguistic challenge as he assimilated to city life.

Most ethnic Chinese who participated in our research, members of the Pontianak's Tio Chu community like Alan, speak in broad conformance with the regime of standard Indonesian. Their speech incorporated few features of what count for them as Malay by provenance, rather than informal in style. Their speech recorded during the research conformed so widely with the regime of the standard that I focus here instead on variable features of Malay, and the "language of Pontianak," as spoken by Malays and Dayaks.

Data in Tables 3.2–3.4 display broad correlations between variable patterns of pronunciations, speakers' ethnicities, and also their biographies as urban natives and newcomers. Aggregated in the bottom row of each are total occasions of use of accent features by Dayaks we recorded, all students and newcomers to Pontianak. Those for ethnic Malays are subgrouped according to speakers' educations and biographies as city natives or newcomers. Malays native to Pontianak are differentiated in the top two rows according to their educational backgrounds. The top row includes data for mostly older persons we recorded who did not graduate from high school (or in some cases middle school). The row below presents data for Malays native to Pontianak and its immediate surround who were graduates from high school and, in most cases, college students. Data in the next row are for Malay students from other parts of the province.

Numbers in cells indicate how many persons in each group used a given proportion of Malay and Indonesian pronunciations in recordings. These are graded by decile from the leftmost column, for those who adopted an entirely vernacular/Malay manners of pronunciation, to the rightmost column for those who used only formal/Indonesian pronunciations. That column also indicates the overall percentage of use of Indonesian pronunciations among members of each group.

Between Ethnicity and Class

Table 3.2 provides evidence of a subethnic "accent" distinction among Malays, keying to socioeconomic class, between (what otherwise counts as) standard Indonesian r and the Malay velar fricative. Although the latter pronunciation can be described as distinctively Malay in that no speaker of any other ethnic group used it in any of our recordings, it was used only infrequently by Malays we recorded; Bambang in this respect was something of an exception.[14] Aside from two older persons who left school early in childhood, the rarity of this pronunciation indicates that its use is less a diacritic of ethnicity than educational and class background among Malays.

Table 3.2 Proportions of r vs. γ Pronunciations
(minimum 90 tokens per speaker)

% Indonesian Speaker group	≥ 0	≥ .1	≥ .2	≥ .3	≥ .4	≥ .5	≥ .6	≥ .7	≥ .8	≥ .9	1	AVG
Native Malay Less Educated ($N = 22$)		2				2	2	2	2	4	8	.8
Native Malay ($N = 25$)					1	1	2	1	2	6	12	.9
Newcomer Malay ($N = 29$)							1	1		3	24	.96
Dayak ($N = 19$)											19	1

Immediate, expressive evidence of this association can be drawn from one of the few instances of velar fricative pronunciations in our recordings, produced by person who was speaking not "in his own voice," but modeling a register of speech he otherwise does not use. This act of speech modeling, like Ina's discussed in Chapter 2, created a temporary shift in interactional alignment in a transitory act of what Agha calls metapragmatic stereotyping (2007: 237). This minor performance during the meeting of a teacher's association is transcribed as Transcript 3.4.

Transcript 3.4 Animating a Stereotype

Untung ndaq ke Komnas HAM dibilang "*guɣu* melakukan pelécéhan séksual."

Lucky (it's not taken) to the National Human Rights Commission and he gets called a "*teacher* engaging in sexual harassment"

To explain his duties, the association's president had presented a scenario in which he might represent a teacher accused of sexual harassment. After describing this situation in somewhat informal Indonesian, he briefly adopted the manner of speech of a hypothetical accuser, referring to the accused as a *guɣu* ('teacher') rather than *guru*. Members of his audience laughed in recognition of the demeanor he assumed in this way: someone who is uneducated or bumpkinish (*kampungan*). They recognized also a shift not between the language of nation and ethnic group, but between the more and less educated.[15]

Between Ethnicity and Style: Central Vowels

Relatively few Indonesian and Malay cognates are pronounced with a final liquid consonant (*l* or *r*) or a glottal stop, respectively. For this reason relatively few examples of pronunciations keying to this contrast in our recordings. But the few data they provide suggest, as the bottom row of Table 3.3 shows, that Dayaks do occasionally adopt the latter pronunciation, albeit far less often than Malays who were native to Pontianak.

Table 3.3 Proportions of Root-Final *l, r* vs. /*q* Usage
(minimum 10 tokens per speaker)

% Indonesian Speaker group	≥ 0	≥ .1	≥ .2	≥ .3	≥ .4	≥ .5	≥ .6	≥ .7	≥ .8	≥ .9	1	AVG
Native less educated (*N* = 16)	9	2		2	1			1		1		.17
Native Malay (*N* = 7)	5	1								1		.14
Newcomer Malay (*N* = 12)	4	1			1	1	1	1	1		2	.42
Dayak (*N* = 10)	1							1	2	3	3	.8

These data also suggest a patterned difference between pronunciations among Malays who are Pontianak natives and newcomers. Less frequent use of a Malay "accent" among newcomers invites attention to the circumstances in which they acquired Indonesian before coming to the city.

Young persons in more rural parts of West Kalimantan, like those in NTT, may acquire Indonesian along with a stronger sense of the diglossic regime of the standard than do Pontianak natives. In this respect the biographies of Dayak newcomers parallel those of their Malay counterparts, who may bring to the city similar orientations to standard Indonesian as distinct from Malay, including "the language of Pontianak."

Support for this conjecture can be drawn from patterned contrasts in pronunciations of central vowels tabulated in Table 3.4 for frequently used deictic and grammatical forms.

Table 3.4 Proportions of *a* vs. *schwa* for Frequently Used Grammatical and Deictic Forms (minimum 30 tokens per speaker)

% Indonesian Speaker group	≥ 0	≥ .1	≥ .2	≥ .3	≥ .4	≥ .5	≥ .6	≥ .7	≥ .8	≥ .9	1	AVG
Native less educated (N = 20)	19	1										
Native educated Malay (N = 23)	20	1	1					1			1	.01
Newcomer Malay (N = 26)	11	2	3	1	2	1	1		2	1	2	.3
Dayak (N = 17)	1		2	1			1	1	6	3	2	.6
adə/ada "there is/are" mana/mana "which (interrogative)" samə/sama "same, equal, with"						-nyə,-ə̃/-nya "associative marker" apə/apa "what (interrogative)" diə/dia "3rd person pronoun"						

In informal settings Malay natives to Pontianak, educated and uneducated alike, almost always spoke their native language. A significant number (6 of 26) of newcomer Malays, on the other hand, showed slight or strong preferences for Indonesian pronunciations. Though usage among Dayaks was overall more variable, all but two had at least occasional recourse to the schwa pronunciation in the interactions we recorded.

These tables radically distance fleeting events of talk from the acts and circumstances in which they occurred. But when aggregated and contrasted in this way, they suggest that persons with different backgrounds adopt different ways of speaking a vernacular of urban modernity. When considered relative to the situations in which they were recorded, on the other hand, they can be interpreted not as examples of biaccentual talk but means for mediating interaction across multiple lines of social difference.

Talk across Lines of Ethnic Difference

Alan's and Bambang's conversation, discussed earlier, was unusual in that they did not adequate their manners of speaking with each other. More common are patterns of syncretic use involving processes of adequation, illustrated here with parts of conversations between Malay and Dayak *mahasiswa*. Examples in Groups 3.3 and 3.4 are drawn from a conversation between Lex (a Dayak) and Bay (a Malay) whose structurally "mixed" verbal demeanors—including "biaccentual" features, transcribed in italic boldface—transiently effaced conditions of ethnic difference.

EXAMPLE GROUP 3.3   LEX (Dayak) to BAY (Malay)

a. Bibitnyə orang jual di manə?
   Where do they sell the seeds?

b. Biasə berap*a* lam*a*?
   Usually how long does it take?

c. Bantai semuə, dah dudok man*e* ingat duni*a* giq, iyə kan?
   They all went along, when they fell into place they didn't remember the world at all, right?

d. Bawaq berap*a* banyak tu biasə tigə hari tu?
   How much [meat] do they take for three days?

EXAMPLE GROUP 3.4   BAY (Malay) to LEX (Dayak)

a. Yang puny*a* anjing tu anoq bagi—apə namə— ratə tulang apə gituq.
   The one who owns the dog gets—what's it called—the bones are divided evenly.

b. Paling jaq berapə? Puloh jut*a* jaq.
   How much at most? Ten million.

Such syncretic registers figure also in interaction that not include ethnic Malays, like the conversation between three Dayaks and a Chinese from which I draw examples in Group 3.5.

EXAMPLE GROUP 3.5   Biaccentual Interaction among Non-Malays

a. Leo: about a conflict involving a mutual acquaintance:
    Aherš ndaq tau berap*a* hari mungkin pihaq datang ke rumah.
    Finally, I don't know how many days, maybe a representative came to
    the house.

b. Barney: responding to a question about the title of a television show:
    Republiq ini maksodš republiq ini Republiq Indonesia lah.
    "Republic" means "Republic" is the Republic of Indonesia.

c. Gerry: about a case of possible corruption:
    Garə-garə Tamrin tu kan, makan duét gaq tu.
    All because of Tamrin, right, he took some money too.

d. David: questioning the possibility of a clock{street light?} having stopped:
    Manə bis*a* mati?
    How could it have been put out?

Leo's use of *ahérš* ("finally") and Barney's of *maksodš* ("the intention, meaning") include a Malay pronunciation of the associative suffix: not *–nyə* but the shorter, more casual nasalized schwa (-š). Leo and Barney are Dayaks whose use can be interpreted, post hoc, as a means for stylistically punctuating assertions they had just made as relevant or true.

Gerry, a native speaker of Khek, made the remark transcribed as 5c to conclude a story he had told, mostly in informal Indonesian, about an investigation that brought down a corrupt politician in Indonesia. He began his concluding remark with a Malay pronunciation of the word *garə-garə*, meaning roughly "all because of." Besides punctuating the end to the tale, this may have lent a more sardonic feel to his story than would have the Indonesian pronunciation (*gara-gara*).

David, a Dayak, posed the skeptical question transcribed as 5d by juxtaposing a "Malay" pronunciation of interrogative *manə* with an Indonesian pronunciation of the predicate *bisa* ("able to"). In use by one non-Malay to others, this phrase illustrates the syncretic vernacular Benny identified more broadly as *bahasa Pontianak*.

Migrants to Pontianak from other parts of Indonesia, like newcomers from other parts of its province, learn to engage the city and its language by incorporating Indonesian and Malay forms in casual manners of speech. Some examples are in Group 3.6, drawn from interaction during which a female researcher of Dayak and Chinese parentage became acquainted with Romi, an ethnic Javanese migrant from Jakarta who had married into another family of Javanese migrants. They chatted outside a parking lot for motorcycles which Romi managed in the middle of town, both making easy recourse to Indonesian and Malay pronunciations of the ubiquitous central vowel.[16]

EXAMPLE GROUP 3.6   Biaccentual Interaction with a
Javanese Migrant

ROMI to Researcher:
Sayə lahér, lahér sayə ni, abang ni lahér di Jakarta.
I was born, I was born, I (elder brother) was born in Jakarta.

Sebenarny*a* dapat istri pun sebenarnyə orang Jawə cuman lahér Pontianak.
Actually, my wife is actually Javanese, but born in Pontianak.

Tapi di atas abang ni masih adə *giq* yang lebéh tu*a giq* kan merantuanyə.
But before me there were others who were older who emigrated.

Researcher to ROMI:
Jadi misalny*a* abang jadi bosnyə kan nantiq adə anaq buah.
So for instance you are the boss here so you have subordinates.

Buk*a* apə?
[They] opened what?

Though radically distanced from the encounters they partially represent, these transcripts illustrate the ways that everyday talk can mediate conditions of ethnic diversity that are a given of life in Pontianak. As some of the city's most educated residents, *mahasiswa* are distinguished also by their uses of Indonesian and English to engage topically with spheres of modernity at large.

Lexicons of Modernity

Mahasiswa in Pontianak, like their counterparts in Kupang, routinely incorporate standard Indonesian and English lexical material into vernacular manners of speech. But these patterns are shaped also by structural commonalities between standard Indonesian and Pontianak Malay, most obviously when pronouncing cognate lexical items ending in final central vowels, like those in Table 3.5.

Table 3.5 Accents in the Lexicon

Lexical Item Indonesian, Malay "gloss"	1. bisa, bisə "to be able"	2. tiga, tigə "three"	3. kerja, kerjə "to work"	4. punya, punyə "to have"	5. cara, carə "manner, Way"	6. acara, acarə "schedule, Agenda"	7. lembaga, lembagə "organization"	8. Indonesia, Indonesiə
Less educated Malays	19/ 412 .04	20/ 293 .06	14/ 250 .05	16/ 101 .14	1/ 19 .05	6/ 16 .27	—	3/ 3 .5
Native educated Malays	80/ 513 .13	30/ 222 .12	39/173 .18	44/ 121 .27	18/ 40 .3	49/ 14 .78	21/ 0	32/ 0
Newcomer educated Malays	137/ 349 .28	84/ 175 .32	55/ 72 .43	49/ 84 .37	33/ 27 .55	18/ 7 .72	19/ 0	8/ 0
Dayak	160/ 88 .64	149/ 32 .8	118/ 26 .82	128/ 19.87	14/ 2 .88	14/ 0 1	3/ 0	25/ 0

Each column is headed by an Indonesian lexical item above its Malay cognate, or a transcription of how it would be pronounced as a Malay word. Numbers of occasions of both kinds of pronunciation in our recordings are tabulated, again according to speakers' ethnic backgrounds and biographies. The first number in each cell indicates how many Indonesian pronunciations (with final /a/) occurred in our recordings, and the second indicates how many pronunciations with schwa. Percentages of Indonesian pronunciations are provided below each pair.

These lexical items figure in speech far less frequently than grammatical and deictic elements, and so there are fewer occasions of use to consider. But those in columns 1–5 do suggest a broadly graded correlation similar to displayed for pronunciations of schwa in Table 3.4. Malays native to Pontianak, regardless of educational background, pronounced these exclusively or predominantly as words of their native language; Malays who were newcomers to Pontianak overall pronounced them slightly more often as in Indonesian. Dayaks pronounced them predominantly but not exclusively as in Indonesian.

Ccolumns 6–8, on the other hand, are headed by semantically and socially distinct lexical items pronounced as Indonesian words by almost all speakers all the time. Semantically they all enable topical engagements with spheres of life that include official (including national) institutions, contexts, and modes of conduct. Correlations of meaning and "accent" are clear from a comparison of columns 5 and 6. The term in column 5, pronounced by some as *cara* and others as *carə*, can be translated as "manner or way of doing something." That in column 6, translatable as "agenda," is associated with issues of official procedure, and was much more commonly pronounced by educated persons as *acara*, in the Indonesian manner. In this way meaning and pronunciation align as they do also for *lembaga* in column 7, meaning "institution" or "organization." It was pronounced by all educated persons as standard Indonesian, often in otherwise vernacular speech. Pronunciations of *Indonesia* are tabulated in column 8 as a kind of limiting case, since one older, less educated Malay's monolingual habits of speech extended to his pronunciation of the name of the nation.

When lexical items of Indonesian provenance figure in otherwise Malay or informal registers of speech, as in Example Group 3.7, they might be called "borrowings." An example would be use of *lembaga* in 7a, a casual remark by a Buginese native of Pontianak to an ethnic Malay. It was similarly used in 7b by one Malay newcomer to another. Both can be compared way with use of *data*,[17] of English provenance, in the otherwise vernacular remark transcribed as 7c.

EXAMPLE GROUP 3.7   Vernacularized Lexical Resources

---

a. Diə kan bukaq lembaga ini Yud, lembaga, lembaga apə ni yə?
   He/she opened an organization, Yud, what kind/model of organization?
b. Karena lembaga beranjaq dari, émbrio munculnyə pertamə xxx lembaga ni.
   Because it began from, the embryo, it first appeared xxx this organization right?
c. Sehinggə yang problèmnyə adalah—oké kitə adə data mintaq, ketike kitə
   So the problem is—OK, we have the data, we ask, when we
   mintaq diyə donor darah kitə kan ndak bise makskəkan kan?
   we ask them to be a blood donor we can't force them/her right?

Example 7c also shows how "foreign" borrowings are commonly vernacularized with the "Malay" associative suffix, in this case by a speaker who chose to use the word *problèm* rather than Indonesian/Malay *soal* (or perhaps the nominal derived from it, *persoalan*). Here English lexical material complements Indonesian in otherwise vernacular, "low" registers of speech.[18]

"Biaccentual" constructions such as *lembaganyə* (8a in Example Group 3.8), *acaranyə* (8b), and *datanyə* (8c) might be disallowed by the regime of the standard, but are common, conspicuous examples of the ways lexical material of standard Indonesian is assimilated to urban registers of speech. Like examples discussed in Chapter 2, they represent a practical effect of Indonesian's unnativeness among educated persons engaged in informal interaction.

EXAMPLE GROUP 3.8 Vernacularized Lexical Resources with the Associative Suffix

a. Terutam*e* kat*ə*kanlah lembag*a* itu lembag*a*ny*ə* bersifat bisnis.
   Above all, say the organization, it's a businesslike organization.
b. Ternyat*ə* SMS tu acar*a*ny*ə* tu di radio gituq ba.
   Turns out (according to) the text message, the event's on the radio.
c. Tapi kelemahaany*ə* adalah datany*ə* kan sepihak.
   But the weakness is that the data is one-sided.

Other data suggest that these assimilative techniques vary as do speakers' ethnic backgrounds and native languages. *Mahasiswa* of all ethnic backgrounds combined Indonesian and English roots (like those in Table 3.6) with the standard Indonesian associative suffix -*nya,* and many also sometimes pronounced that suffix as in "Malay." But only ethnic Malays pronounced that suffix as in their native language in combination with lexical material of English provenance. This might testify to variability in syncretic use that indirectly and unobviously reflects their ethnic backgrounds.

Table 3.6 Indonesian and English Lexicons in Vernacular Constructions

# Occasions of Pronunciation with:	Indonesian -*nya*	Malay -*ny*ə / speaker's ethnicity
Indonesian Provenance		
acara (agenda)	4	4 / All Malay
panitia (organizing committee)	2	5 / All Malay
kendala (obstacle, issue)	3	7 / All Malay
English Provenance		
f/pungsi (function)	1	5 / 4 Malay, 1 Migrant
kuwalitas (quality)	12	7 / All Malay
kondisi (condition)	2	8 / All Malay
sistèm (system)	6	9 / All Malay
data (data)	5	11 / All Malay

Social Biographies and Linguistic Alignments

The other-than-standard Indonesians spoken among *mahasiswa* in Pontianak are integral to urban life, and instrumental for dealing with topics partaking of the national. That they vary more than their analogs in Kupang can be seen as a result of the greater salience of ethnic conditions in Pontianak. But they are similarly enabled by a bracketing of the regime of the standard. For this reason they invite the same question taken up in chapter two: how is that regime understood and valued by persons who flout it in such routine, obvious ways?

This question can be approached by again considering responses to queries during semi-structured interviews, although circumstances in Pontianak and West Kalimantan limited our ability to find interviewees from a wide range of salient ethnic backgrounds. We were only able to interview comparable numbers of young, educated Chinese speakers of Tio Chu, ethnic Dayaks, and ethnic Malays native to Pontianak. All were interviewed by young persons of similar ethnic background. We were unable to arrange comparable numbers of interviews with speakers of Khèk, with Malay newcomers to Pontianak, or with any members of any of the migrant groups now residing there.

Table 3.7 summarizes their responses to some of the same queries discussed in Chapter 2. In Pontianak, however, interviewees were first asked whether they "controlled the general/common language of this town" (*menguasai bahasa umum kota ini*). We used this phrase to avoid introducing right away a distinction between Malay as a language of the ethnoregion (*bahasa Melayu*) and a vernacular spoken in the city (*bahasa Pontianak*).

This choice of phrase may have led 4 of 16 Malay respondents to describe their command of "the town's language" as only fair but all later reported, as did their co-ethnics, that they spoke Malay in most or all of the hypothetical scenarios presented. Ten of 15 Dayak interviewees described themselves as having strong or fair abilities in "the town's language," whereas only 6 of 15 Chinese (all Pontianak natives) did so. To evaluate these responses I tabulate them with two pairs of numbers. Numbers before a slash indicate how many in each group reported themselves to be fluent or to have fair ability in the language of the city. Numbers after a slash indicate how many of these persons later reported using "the language of city" in at least one hypothetical scenario. This demonstrates apparent discrepancies between responses—for 2 of 6 Chinese, and 3 of 10 Dayaks—that might be grounds for doubting the accuracy of one or both.

Table 3.7 Responses to Queries

	Chinese (N = 15) 8 M, 7 F	Dayak (N = 18) 11 M, 7 F	Malay (N = 16) 9M, 7F
Reports of Competence			
Malay: Fluent	4/2	5/2	9
Fair	2/0	5/1	7
(# reporting competence / # later reporting use)			
Indonesian:			
Fluent	8	16	8
Fair	4	2	4
Reports of Use			
1. Most frequently used?	Indonesian: 8 Malay: 0	Indonesian: 9 Malay: 1	Indonesian: 2 Malay: 14
2. Used with a friend of different ethnicity?	Indonesian: 12 Malay: 2	Indonesian: 18 Malay: 0	Indonesian: 11 Malay: 5
Responses to Queries			
3. # affirming the statement "Young people in this town can generally speak good Indonesian."	8 (.5)	13 (.7)	15 (.9)
4. # affirmative replies to query "Have you ever felt awkward speaking Indonesian?"	9 (.6)	17 (.9)	14 (.9)
5. # reporting fluent Indonesian and answering "yes" to query 4	3 (of 8)	13 (of 16)	7 (of 8)

Note: M = male; F = female.

Alternatively, these responses can be evaluated as reflecting different language-linked senses of group membership. A query not about a named language but a place ("talk in the city") may have oriented them less to issues of language competence than capacities to engage with urban life. Questions which directed their attention to particular kinds of context, on the other hand, could elicit reports oriented to acts of speech, and so also the received distinction between Indonesian and native languages of an ethnic outgroup. Notable is the absence of such "inconsistencies" in responses to these queries from Malay interviewees.

Interviewees' ethnic backgrounds can be seen to correlate with their reactions to the statement (also discussed also in Chapter 2) that "Young people in this town can generally speak good Indonesian."[19] Disagreement was commoner among Chinese interviewees, suggesting a stronger orientation to the regime of the standard and Indonesian's distinctness from Malay. In this way the salience of Indonesian's unnativeness can be seen as stronger for citizens without a native ethnoregion.[20]

We were only able to interview a small number of Tio Ciu speakers, and their responses to query 4—"Have you ever felt awkward speaking Indonesian?"—only provide weak support for the supposition that their standard Indonesian competences are relatively strong in comparison with others, including ethnic Malays. But taken together with their self-reports of competence, they reflect a broadly different stance to standard Indonesian which is evident also in responses summarized in row 5. 3 of 8 Chinese who had described themselves as fluent in Indonesian later recounted experiences of dysfluency; only 1 of 8 Malays who had previously described themselves as fluent in Indonesian did not. Taken together, these responses suggest a stronger orientation to Indonesian's distinctness among Chinese than Malays.

Dayak self-reports of competence in standard Indonesian may also seem inconsistent with their responses to query 4, but should be considered along with their descriptions of circumstances in which they felt awkward, most reflecting their newcomer status. Some, rather like their Kupang counterparts, found on arrival in Pontianak that they needed to reduce transfer effects from their native languages which marked their ethnic background. (See, for instance, remarks by MAH in Appendix 3.3.) Others described encounters with native speakers of other languages earlier in life when they traveled within the interior of West Kalimantan to attend secondary schools (one was JON, also quoted in Appendix 3.3). Their prior mobility enabled and obliged them to modify their ways of speaking Indonesian before going to Pontianak.

In the absence of interviews with Malay newcomers to Pontianak, I can only conjecture that they acquired Indonesian competences primarily in educational contexts along with practices of literacy and stronger orientations to the regime of the standard. Certainly while in Pontianak they modify native habits of speech they adopt "back home" (the districts of Sambas, Landak, Ketapang, and Ulu Kapuas). For them, the dialect of Pontianak (*bahasa Melayu Pontianak*) is more appropriate in that city, but not "better" or more "modern." Comparability between these dialects is evident when persons from the same region address each other in its distinctive dialect, sometimes in the presence of others with whom they use Pontianak Malay.[21] Intraprovincial parity between varieties of Malay was also evinced by Malays native to Pontianak during interviews when they spontaneously described competences in other varieties of the language, acquired while living elsewhere in the province.

Taken together, responses to these queries suggest that orientations to the regime of standard Indonesian differ with interviewees' ethnicities and biographies. Though the unnative linguistic forms they acquire are the same, their uses are informed by different, changeable senses of the standard's distinctness. This includes the ways they can or should not be syncretized to vernacular speech. In this way an absence of Indonesian native speakers enables multiple modes of verbal engagement with urban life.

On the Intimacy of Mixed Messages

In Chapter 2, I interpreted some uses of Kupang's vernacular as having the capacity to engender senses of cultural intimacy in interaction. I suggested, along lines developed by Michael Herzfeld, that these could emerge in conspicuously "mixed" conversational dynamics among persons who shared awareness of the regime of the standard as they jointly flouted it. A similar interpretation is invited by an exchange like that reproduced as Transcript 3.5, drawn from the beginning of a conversation between two young, previously unacquainted, educated Malays in Pontianak. It occurred in the government office where our interviewer, Yud, asked Mus, a civil servant, about his official duties.

Transcript 3.5 Opening an Interview

Mus: Nantiq kitə kan adə ini adə	Mus: Later we, there's a, a
pertemuan jugaq xx rifiu	meeting xxxx a review
tentang pekerjaan kitε.	about our work.
Ha kaloq misaləǝ̃ bagus,	So if for instance it's good
kontraqə̃ dilanjutkan . . .	the contract will be extended.
Yud: Oh adə penilaian?	Yud: Oh, so there's a review?

Mus's Malay "accent" was evident when he said *kitə* ("we") and *adə* (there is),and when he attached the Malay associative suffix to *misal* ("example") and *kontraq* ("contract"). Following up with a query about what Mus called a *rifiu*, "review"— pronounced with an "f," marking its foreign provenance—Yud combined Malay *adə* with an Indonesian nominal synonymous with that English borrowing (*penilaian*, formed from the root *nilai*, "evaluate").

Meeting for the first time in an official setting, and speaking of official matters, two educated Indonesians might be expected to at least begin their conversation with standard, "high" Indonesian, and in conformance with the regime of the standard. By diverging early and markedly from that regime, these two young men can be seen to have engaged in a mutual project of adequation, each talking so as to corroborate the other's "tactics of intersubjectivity" (Bucholtz and Hall 2005: 599). A sense of solidarity, if not intimacy, could arise from the disjunction thus created between their commonality as educated Indonesians on one hand, and as co-ethnics on the other. The ethnopolitical context sketched earlier might have likewise lent salience to the "Malay" quality of an otherwise topically and contextually Indonesian conversation.

Other kinds of vernacular usage could engender similar sentiments of mutuality between persons whose biographies and language competences differ. Like their counterparts in Kupang, for instance, newcomers to Pontianak might speak and evaluate others' speech in ways that presuppose shared awareness of the regime of the standard. Like Ina and her newcomer friends, they might have a tacit sense that back home their talk might sound like "bad Indonesian," or, perhaps, ethnic Malay. In the ears of persons outside the town, talk like Leo's, Barney's, and Dave's might be heard as evidence that in Pontianak they have acquired a "Malay accent."

The urban character of that vernacular, neither national or ethnic, could in this way derive situated values that differ for members of communities of practice in this ethnically and linguistically diverse urban center. Unnative elements of anonymous Indonesian could then gain expressive values from registers of vernacular speech, and the tactics of intersubjectivity in which they commonly figure.

An Enabling Absence

The other-than-standard Indonesians discussed here are identified by some as *bahasa Pontianak*, but this label is less widely recognized than its analog in Kupang (*bahasa Kupang*). This might be partly because vernacular registers of speech in Pontianak incorporate elements of a politically salient ethnoregional language. I have suggested here that their variability, at least among some young residents, gives them multiple roles in a broader integrative dynamic. Pontianak's vernacular may not circulate far beyond the city's ambit, like *bahasa Kupang*. But Pontianak's young, educated residents similarly appropriate unnative Indonesian to local projects of modernity which are enabled, but not determined, by the regime of the standard. In Pontianak more than Kupang, Indonesian's radical anonymity enables "social-semiotic moves," as Eckert puts it, that allow members of communities of practice to "reinterpret [. . .] variables and combin[e] and recombin[e] them in a continual process of bricolage" (2012: 94).

This very partial sketch, together with that in Chapter 2, provides two different perspectives which help in Chapter 4 to revisit Goenawan's paradox with broader terms, and to consider how a plurality of other-than-standard Indonesians might engender senses of national belonging among those who speak them.

Notes

CHAPTER 3

1. In total about 200 students took part in our research, both as participants in interactions we recorded or in interviews, conducted both formally and informally.

2. By one estimate, Pontianak was already home to 10,000 Chinese and 3,000 Malays in the early nineteenth century (Leyden 1837: 105a).

3. "[O]rang Dayak menjadi buruh di tanah sendiri . . . kerusakan alam . . . juga memporakporandakan kehidupan social masyarakat adat Dayak. Tak terhitung lagi konflik-konflik besar dan kecil antara masyarakat déngan pengusaha dan bahkan déngan sesama anggota masyarakat."

4. These schools were under the sponsorship of a Catholic NGO (Yayasan Karya Sosial Pancur Kasih).

5. On Malay dialects of the island of Borneo, see Collins (1990, 1991, 2006). Relations between Indonesian and dialects spoken in other parts of West Kalimantan, as well as Sarawak and Sabah, are too complex to be surveyed here. Kartinnen observes that "[i]n spite of Malay's deep roots in Borneo some people identify its origin with the neighboring country of Malaysia. The sense of Malay as a 'foreign' language may reflect resource conflicts in the past, but above all it suggests that kinship and trade relations, rather than overarching political institutions, constituted the principal framework for social integration in precolonial times" (2005: 276–277). See also Aman and Mustaffa (2009); Hoogevorst (2011); and Wong Kon Ling (2000).

6. On the Madurese/Dayak conflict, see Sudagung (2001); M. Hawkins (2009); B. Subianto (2009); Davidson (2007, 2008); Peluso and Harwell (2001); van Klinken (2007); and Rosdiawan (2007).

7. Na'im and Syaputra 2011. According to data from the 2010 census reported by IPAC (2018), 18.5% are ethnic Malay, and 7.8% are Javanese. Rahmawati and Batuallo (2007) estimate that 90,000 Kenayatn Dayaks live in the regency of Pontianak.

8. See Tanasaldy (2007, 2012). A public image of this relation can be seen in a tableau outside a shopping mall that opened in 2007 (for a picture, see Davidson 2008: 170), consisting of three male figures distinguished by clothing and accoutrements as ethnically Malay, Chinese, and Dayak. The inscription describes this as *Etnis Dalam Harmonis*, "Ethnicities in Harmony." Words of English provenance might have been

chosen to signal a new era of relations, and perhaps to avoid otherwise sensitive choices such as between the Indonesian words *suku* (tribe) and *bangsa* (nation).

9. Four respondents reported being offspring of "mixed" Chinese and Dayak parentage, and just one described his parents as Malay and Chinese. Three of 12 migrants we interviewed described themselves as Pontianak natives, and 5 claimed fluency in an ethnic language other than Malay. For further discussions of the ambiguities of Malay and Buginese identities, see Carruthers (2017a, 2017b, 2018).

10. The conversation was found among 76 hours of recordings, involving 150 speakers in 119 different situations.

11. "Pernah, omong déngan itulah orang-orang yang—istilah dari Jakarta gitu, jadi kita itu bingung. Ndak fasihlah *bisə* omongnya tapi kaku gitu ndak fasih kaya orang *biasənyə* . . . ya bahasa kita ngomongnya, bahasa omong '*mo ke manə?*' Eh lupa '*mo ke manə*' ndak ngerti kan? '*Ko mo ke manə*' *Manə* jadi kita gunakan bahasa Indonésialah, yang baik ngertilah tapi itulah seperti harus pikir dulu, lah bahasa Indonésia pikir dulu 'oh bahasa Indonésia yang bener gimana ya,' supaya itu orang mengerti kan gitu . . . salah omong. Orang pikir *gilə* ha ini orang *gilə* lah . . . orang ndak ngerti sedikit dibilang *gilə*."

12. Jessica Birnie-Smith (2018) provides a far more detailed account of usage among young Khek and Tio Ciu residents.

13. Preferences for use of *saja* versus *aja* were strongest among ethnic Malay newcomers to Pontianak (40 vs. 10), followed by Dayaks (13 vs. 36) and ethnic Malays native to Pontianak (3 vs. 53).

14. A third of these occasions of use of /ɣ/ by educated Malays occurred when saying the word meaning "person," *oɣang*, perhaps carrying an expressive feel like the use of "guy" in English.

15. Aman and Mustaffa (2009) document parallel developments of the velar fricative as a shibboleth of intra-ethnic class difference in Kuching, a city in Sarawak.

16. Romi pronounced central vowels with Indonesian *a* on 300 of 686 occasions; our researcher 84 of 472.

17. Native speakers of English commonly pronounce the second, unstressed vowel of "data" as schwa; Indonesians, including native speakers of Malay, pronounce the second syllable with final *a*.

18. A rough indication of knowledge of English among educated persons in Pontianak we worked with can be drawn from reports of competence provided by 65 of them during interviews. Thirty described their English reading abilities as fair, and 9 as fluent; 19 claimed fair and one claimed advanced comprehension of spoken English; 27 claimed fair and 5 claimed good abilities to write English; only 15 described their spoken English as fair.

19. "Kaum muda di kota ini pada umumnya bisa berbahasa Indonésia dengan baik."

20. Anecdotal remarks made during the research suggest that some young Chinese use Jakarta's vernacular, not Pontianak's, in such situations. They reportedly acquire

facility in Jakarta's vernacular during long stays in that city with relatives, many refugees from Pontianak after race riots in the 1960s (see Hui 2011: 24). Weak corroboration of these reports from interviews, discussed later, is that five Chinese interviewees initially reported themselves to be fluent in *bahasa Jakarta*. However, only one later reported using it in any interactional scenario presented.

21. This occurred, for instance, during a meeting of persons of diverse backgrounds that included two Malays from Sambas. One addressed the other as follows:

> Sebenarny*é* say*é* bis*é* semboh batok say*é* kalau ndaq minum kopi.
> Actually I can get over cough my if (I) don't drink coffee.

He used the distinctively Sambas pronunciation of final vowels transcribed as *é*, pronounced roughly like the first part of the vowel in the standard American pronunciation of the word *say*. In Pontianak Malay that vowel would be pronounced as schwa:

Sebenarny*ə* say*ə* bis*ə* semboh batok say*ə* kalau ndak minum kopi.

And in standard Indonesian it would be pronounced with a vowel more like that in the first syllable of standard American "father."

Sebenarny*a* say*a* bis*a* semboh batok say*a* kalau ndak minum kopi.

An overview of the Pontianak dialect of Malay is provided by Kamal et al. (1986). A sketch of the Sambas dialect, touched on earlier, is in Kamal et al. (1984) and Susilo Firman (1998).

4   A PLURAL UNITY

Kupang and Pontianak are just two among scores of Middle Indonesian locales, and not necessarily remarkable scenes of ethnic or linguistic diversity. This sketch of Indonesian's role in lives of their educated residents helps to gauge the value and limits of the regime of the standard language. Empirical particulars demonstrate what it enables, but does not determine, in otherwise different sociolinguistic dynamics. Here they help generalize to an alternative account of the values of the paradox Indonesian contains.

An emblematic expression of that paradox might be Indonesia's motto, the Old Javanese phrase *Bhinnéka tunggal ika*. This can be translated directly as "Different/split that, united that"[1] but is more commonly translated (reversing the order of its words) as "Unity in diversity" or (tacitly echoing the motto of the United States) "Out of many, one." This latter translation intimates an integrative process in which languages other than unified, unifying Indonesian become subordinate and perhaps residual.

I have suggested here that Indonesian is itself becoming plural in its role as a mediator between hundreds of languages which were otherwise largely unrelated to each other before the advent of the nation. So too this linguistic diversity can be identified now as a condition of linguistic plurality insofar as they are now recognized, individually and collectively, as comparably ethnoregional. In this case chapters 2 and 3 can be seen as documenting some of plural character Indonesian has developed as its has been assimilated to diverse locales and language competences.

This perspective can be extended with a newer, darker story of sociolinguistic change, telling of Indonesian as a threat to that antecedent linguistic diversity. This helps here to consider why global English, in turn, is a perceived threat to standard Indonesian. Positioning Indonesian in this way, between the ethnoregional and global, provides

Other Indonesians. Joseph Errington, Oxford University Press. © Oxford University Press 2022.
DOI: 10.1093/oso/9780197563670.003.0004

context for revisiting Cornelis Lay's observations, quoted in chapter 1, about the plural character that now distinguishes the Indonesian nation.

This argument has two elements. One draws on Anderson's description of national languages generally, and Indonesia particularly, as one among the "last wave" of postcolonial nations. The other, located beyond and below hierarchies which are central to Anderson's account, centers on Herzfeld's notion of "cultural intimacy," the interpretive device I borrowed to present transcriptions of a few interactional events. Both essays about nationalism take up issues of language, and provide complementary angles of vision on unnative Indonesian, as an enabler of its speakers' ambient awarenesses or imaginings of each other, in and with the nation.

The distinctness of the Indonesian paradox can be considered, finally, with an eye to sociolinguistic dynamics elsewhere, moving from what now counts as the Global South to ostensibly monoglot nations of Western Europe in the Global North. Woolard's account of Catalan and Castillian, languages in a relation broadly similar to that between Indonesian and Malay, offers here grounds for comparing young bilinguals in Spain with *mahasiswa* in Indonesian towns. Now that languages of other European nations are destandardizing, they can be considered briefly as potentially analogous with Indonesian. Finally, what I call the plurality of Indonesians in its nation can be juxtaposed to recent, rapidly expanding conditions in European cities now identified as "superdiverse."

Together, these three quick comparisons suggest a revised version of the developmentalist narrative about Indonesian, framed in the Cold War, about a state-driven effort in a Third World nation to emulate the modernity of the First World. Now Indonesian's plural condition allows for a story in which it might be a harbinger for other nations' ongoing linguistic engagements with globalization.

Diversity, Endangerment, and Salad Language

Kupang and Pontianak were introduced as peripheral and provincial "blind spots" for the diglossic regime of the standard, and everyday manners of speech in both were analogized to what Moeliono dubbed the "Jakartan dialect of Indonesian." Because of their urban character they elude the national/ethnoregional binary, and count as peripheral examples of the nation's linguistic diversity (*kebinékaan bahasa*).

Some working for the New Order regarded ethnic and linguistic diversity as a legacy of the past to be superseded; now it is more widely seen as a source of value under threat. Ethnoregional languages are now often identified in popular media as "threatened with extinction" (*terancam punah*), in "their death throes" (*sekarat*), or as being "killed" (*dibunuh*) (see, e.g., Nino Histiraludin 2012; Sapto Pradityo 2015; and Amar Ola Keda 2018). These undesired consequences of modernization are thematic in stories about small, peripheral communities, and sometimes provoke calls for closer adherence to the regime of the standard. Observing anonymous standard Indonesian's functional distinctness would ensure the distinctness and safety of authentic, native (*asli*) languages.

This narrative lacks fit, however, among members of communities who have little sense of the "authenticity" of their native manners of speech. In the absence of native speakers of Indonesian, for instance, speakers of Kui and Sumbawan in NTT are shifting to what is for them the "freely-chosen language of unity among all ethnic groups" (see Shiohara 2010, 2012). They can acquire Indonesian competences without internalizing a sense that they are "minority language speakers [with a] . . . mother language [that is] being displaced" (Shiohara 2012: 120). Jenny Zhang and Regina Yanti (2019) similarly describe communities in NTT whose residents harbor no assumption that there is a "natural" connection need between their languages, communities, and cultural traditions.

Secondly, and more broadly, widely circulating stories of language death exclude patterns of speech like those sketched here. These are peripheralized even as they circulate beyond urban centers and give rise to what Simon Musgrave calls "shifts in patterns of multilingualism" (2014: 101).

Kupang and NTT provide one example of the ways that circuits of intraprovincial mobility enable an urban vernacular to become one of what Subahn Zein identifies as 43 regional lingua francas that "connect people at the regional level (i.e., between villages, communities, regencies, provinces)" (2020: 34, quoting Nahir 1984). Of these 14, including Kupang Malay, are distinctly "Malayic or indigenized varieties of Malay/Indonesian" (2020: 34)

> [that] are increasingly urban. Cities such as Ambon, Kupang and Manado have become melting pots of ethnicities where younger generations, thanks to advances in transportation can now travel easily . . . while acquiring indigenized varieties of Malay in the process. . . . The dissemination of these Malay regional lingua francas . . . [is] allowing them to be acquired even by non-literate populations. (Zein 2020: 36)

The more they circulate beyond urban centers, the more these vernaculars, rather than standard Indonesian, pose a proximate "threat" to local languages. John Bowden (2012a, 2012b) notes this dynamic in connection with the "displacement" of ethnoregional languages in NTT and the province of North Maluku (Maluku Utara):

> [m]any people assume that when Indonesians give up their former native vernaculars, they replace these local languages with "Indonesian," and thus imply that local linguistic emblems are lost in the process of language shift as people move to a nationalistic mode of communication. In reality, however, most communities are shifting to one of the varieties of local Malay and not really to "Indonesian" at all, at least not as a home language. (Bowden 2012a)

Standard Indonesian's syncretization with local languages, including varieties of Malay, can lead to what Bowden (2012a) calls "nationalistic mode[s] of communication," which in turn contribute to the plural character of Indonesian. Under the diglossic regime these regional lingua francas[2] appear to be residual elements in dynamics of language shift or death. This can be seen in views of language change not just in peripheral communities but urban centers like Pontianak.

In 2018 Dedy Ari Asfar, representing Pontianak's *Balai Bahasa* (House of Language), described threats to ethnoregional languages of West Kalimantan arising not from governmental policy (*kebijaqan pemerintah*), but rather the desires and motivations of "us [Indonesians] (*kita sendiri*)" (Ridhoino Kristo Sebastianus Melano 2018). In his view this is due to feelings of embarrassment among newcomers to the city if they are heard speaking languages native to their rural communities (*désa*), even with members of their own families. Were those languages firmly defended (*tetap terjaga*) in family circles (*lingkungan keluarga*), he observed, then use of Indonesian would be restricted to its proper domains and formal contexts (*kontèks formal*). He thus invoked the diglossic norm as a defense against language shift, and in so doing excluded from his scenario the other-than-standard Indonesians sketched in Chapter 3, which as a matter of practice figure more widely than the standard in a wide range of extrafamilial, informal interactions.

In 2011 Ibu Evi Novianti, also of the *Balai Bahasa*, called attention to what she called the uncertain future of ethnoregional Malay as spoken natively in Pontianak (*nasib bahasa Melayu Pontianak*). To document linguistic effects of the town's changing demographics she compared features of everyday speech of newcomers and migrants (*pendatang*) on one hand, and Pontianak's original residents (*penduduk asli*), on the other. Absent from the contrasts she identifies is that between Indonesian velar stop /g/ and the Malay velar fricative /ɣ/.

She diagnosed these differences as resulting not from newcomers' disinclinations to emulate ethnic Malays, but their lack of familiarity with native Malay vocabulary and terms (*kosa kata dan istilah*). They do in fact seek "to fit in with their new situation . . . [and] use Pontianak Malay in interaction with urban natives. However, the Malay they use is not true Malay but Indonesian with a dialect of Malay"[3] (Evi Novianti 2011: 71). She alludes here also to vernacular registers of speech like those described in Chapter 3, but not their value for such persons as means for adequating interactional relations across lines of ethnic difference. Both scenarios residualize (in different ways) structurally "mixed" registers of speech. Their values go unrecognized in both scenarios because they are connected expressively to communities of practice, not emblematically to extrinsically identified social groups.

Similar dynamics are now identified by some as threatening to the much "larger" Javanese language. An analysis of data from recent censuses in Central and East Java leads Ravindranath and Cohn (2014) to suggest that speakers of Javanese living in these relatively homogeneous provinces associate Indonesian with their co-ethnics as much as with outsiders. This is evident from the commonplace ways both languages are syncretized to what was first called in Javanese "salad language" (*bahasa gado-gado*).

These registers of speech incorporate bivalent and cognate elements of both languages. Even when speaking informally, in "low" Javanese, educated Javanese make easy recourse to Indonesian and English lexicons, like their counterparts in Kupang and Pontianak (Errington 1998b: 98–116).[4] Newcomers to Java commonly acquire other-than-standard registers of "salad language" for purposes of interethnic communication (Goebel (2010a, 2010b). Tamtamo (2018a, 2018b) likewise describes "patterns of bilingual combination" that distinguish everyday interaction among Javanese high school students, and that regularly "blur the boundaries of national and local language" (2018a: 180).

Whether or not they represent a threat to Javanese, these other-than-standard registers of "salad language" broadly resemble those described here. Kupang and Pontianak appear in this context as two among many scenes of pluralizing dynamics. In both towns varieties of Indonesian are emerging that differ as do their populations and regions, but that are enabled and united under the regime of the standard.

This raises the question of how a plurality of Indonesians, so widespread and different from the emblematic standard, might enable Indonesian speakers' senses of national belonging or unity.

Imaged Languages in Imagined Communities

Widespread, visible slippage between vernacular practice and official norm appears to some as lessening Indonesian's value as an emblem or flag for what Michael Billig calls the banality of its nation (1995: 8). What kind of ambient awareness can Indonesians have of each other if they speak "the same" national language so differently and in ways that are so clearly not "good and true"?

Two of Anderson's broad insights into print-literate languages and imagined national communities provide part of a possible answer. One is the way languages enable members of nations to engage the condition of human mortality; another is about the modularity of national imaginings, which he identifies in nationalisms that began as elite responses to different political and cultural crises over four centuries, around the world.

Anderson suggests that native languages have existential value for their native speakers' quasi-transcendental senses of sharedness. When native competences are understood to be a common, natural condition of fatedness, then a "mother tongue" counts as an inheritance from dead national predecessors that is bequeathed to one's successors. While narratives of nationhood provide senses of historical continuity, the condition of native speakership represents a mode of existential connection across generations.

Anderson's argument hinges also on the role played by print technology in the fostering of senses of connectedness among national contemporaries, those one knows of or imagines as living at the same time as oneself. Print made this possible in early modern Europe, in his view, when written texts, and their languages, became commodities. Orthographic representations of language then became enmeshed with the market, as printers sought to maximize the legibility of texts for readers whose manners of speaking might vary widely. Economic and semiotic advantages converged as texts circulated widely irrespective of readers' different spoken dialects.

In this way, Anderson observes, engagements with literate language came to presuppose readers' shared awarenesses of the "steady, anonymous, simultaneous activity" (Anderson 1991: 26) of their national contemporaries. They came to be known not "directly" through experience and speech, but in senses of "deep horizontal comradeship" grounded in the "silent privacy" of "acts of reading" (Anderson 1991: 35).

Anderson notes in passing the collateral effect of print-literate languages on manners of speaking which lose "caste" (1991: 45) relative to their higher status "cousins." This is because print-imaged languages are necessarily "far fewer" than the "idiolects" they subsume (1991: 42–43). But he passes over the ways that images of native speakership can naturalize these hierarchies, or linguistic "castes," touched on briefly in Chapter 1. His world-historical concerns lead him to focus instead on transitions between the first national imaginings, which emerged in the New World, to Western Europe, Eastern Europe, and finally formerly colonized parts of the world. Different modes of nationalism emerged, he argues, as elite responses to different political and existential crises.

Indonesia has a special place in Anderson's account of "the last wave" of postcolonial nationalisms. It began, as noted in Chapter 1, among members of the subaltern elite of the Netherlands East Indies: members of the dominated fraction of the dominant segment of imperial society. It is significant for Anderson's argument that they devised an official mode of nationalism by pirating anonymous, print-literate Malay. That Indonesian had become a "mother tongue" of some Indonesians by the 1980s served in his broader argument that an official nationalism was being superceded by a popular mode of nationalism.

When the internal plurality of Indonesian is brought into view, however, so are broader questions about the relation between social and linguistic hierarchies on one hand, and subjective senses of national belonging on the other. Eric Hobsbawm identified the limits of elite-focused approaches to nationalism by pointing to the gap between agendas of "spokesmen and activists" (1990: 11) for nationalisms on one hand, and on the other "what is in the minds of . . . citizens" who may or not identify themselves as "constitut[ing] the social being" (1990: 11) of the nation.

This observation rings true for the top-down, state-driven success story of Indonesian development; it calls attention also to the ambiguous position in national society that is occupied by *mahasiswa*. As distinctly educated persons in sustained engagement with the standard language they might be exponents of what he calls "national propaganda," and among the nation's "most loyal citizens or supporters" (1990: 11). Yet they habitually speak in ways that diverge from the norms supported by that propaganda, and distance themselves from official images of the "social being" of the nation.

This disjunction or gap can be taken up more ethnographically along lines suggested by Michael Herzfeld.

Hierarchy and Intimacy

Middle Indonesian towns are peripheral relative to Jakarta, and most of their residents are peripheral relative to the foremost of Hobsbawm's spokesmen and agents for the national agenda. Herzfeld helped earlier to frame that condition of peripherality as it figured in interaction that might have enabled situated senses of cultural intimacy. This was easy to do because his notion of cultural intimacy rests on a broad analogy between linguistic hierarchies (diglossia) and broader sociosemiotic hierarchies he identifies with the term disemia.

Research on Crete led Herzfeld to "disemia" as a rubric for symbolic representations that legitimize hierarchical and geosocial relations between centers and peripheries. He developed an account of these "high" and "low" symbolic domains with an analogy to distinctions between "high" and "low" languages in diglossic situations. In peripheral communities he observed senses of cultural intimacy emerging among persons whose joint awareness of "high" norms and symbols figured in conduct that flouted those norms. Cultural intimacy in this way emerges as quality of copresence that is created, quasi-collusively, with techniques for parodizing official symbols and norms to express "popular irony at the expense of the powerful" (1997: 14). Disemia extends to language hierarchies, he observes, through use of "social dialects" that are "flaw[ed] and imperfect" (1997: 172) to engender senses of "privacy." This privacy rests on awareness and exclusion of otherwise anonymous contemporaries who occupy the condition Michael Warner (2002: 56) calls "stranger sociability," known of as sharers of norms but not through interactional experience.

Herzfeld's passing remark on dialects fits well some of the "mixed" talk described here. Shared awareness of the regime of the standard figured directly in Ina's parodic report of what folks back home say about her "bad Indonesian," and invited shared intimacy from her fellow newcomers to Kupang. When the highly educated Miriam and Halle shifted casually and jointly between Indonesian and English in otherwise vernacular interaction, they enacted a doubly shared and distinct position as Kupang residents versed in two print-literate languages of modernity. Examples of biaccentual usage in Pontianak—not quite Indonesian, not exactly Malay—were likewise interpreted as enabling previously unacquainted co-ethnics to cultivate transient senses of intimacy in a distinctly Indonesian context, and in discussion of distinctly Indonesian topics. Their collaborative conduct, acknowledging and diverging from the standard, engendered what Herzfeld calls a "fellowship of the flawed" (1997: 28) between fellow citizens and fellow Malays.

Contemporaries and Consociates

Anderson and Herzfeld thematized the linguistic grounds of national belonging from two different perspectives. Anderson identifies the relation of standard languages to ambient awarenesses of otherwise anonymous fellow citizens; the unnativeness of Indonesian in this context can be seen as enabling maximally abstract "cultural images" (Irvine 1990) or "stereotypes" (Agha 2007) of fellow speakers. Herzfeld, on the other hand, situates the "high" standard, along with "low" vernaculars, in expressively immediate social engagements, with cultural intimacy emergent as a "phenomenological property of social life." (Appadurai 1995: 208) These complementary views help here to frame Indonesian's plural unity in broader terms, and in a dynamic interplay between linguistic typifications (or imaginings) and interactional experiences of social others. To throw this interplay into relief I summarized Anderson's and Herzfeld's arguments with terms drawn from Alfred Schutz's writings on the phenomenology of social life (1978). His ideal-typical approach is too abstract to offer direct purchase on questions of political culture, but for the same reason his distinctions are broad enough to consider Anderson's and Herzfeld's accounts together.

I summarized Anderson's observations on the transcendence of national languages with a distinction Schutz's draws between persons who are known as "predecessors" and "successors." These are persons who are typified or imagined, but never known "directly," relative to one's own condition of mortality, and whom Anderson identifies as imagined fellow members of a transcendent national community. The term "contemporary" was adapted from Schutz to describe others who are known through social typifications, but not direct experience, to be living at the same time as oneself. It helped here summarize Anderson's observations on relations between readers of print-imaged languages and their absent, anonymous fellow readers.

To these three categories Schutz added a fourth which helps reframe Herzfeld's notion of cultural intimacy. "Consociates," for Schutz, are those among one's contemporaries who can be known "directly" in transient conditions of experiential sharedness. In these spaces of lived time, and talk, consociates know each other as "growing old together," as Schutz puts it. These experiences are grounds, in turn, for the greater or lesser "vividness" that accrues to typifications of social others.

Framed in these terms, cultural intimacy emerges in experiences of consociateship which incorporate shared awareness of anonymous contemporaries. In Chapters 2 and 3 these were situations in which, by virtue of shared knowledge of context, joint use of vernacular speech among consociates presupposed also shared awareness of standard-speaking contemporaries. Cultural intimacy emerges from this both/and orientation that different varieties of "mixed use" can mark and mediate, depending on context and individuals' biographies.

Fluid orientations to contemporaries and consociates could be read also from seemingly inconsistent responses to queries by interviewees who affirmed their fluency in Indonesian, but described occasions when they lacked it. I framed these as presupposing different ideas (or typifications) of "the Indonesian language." Initial queries about competence, posed without reference to interactional setting or experience, tacitly invited their self-identification with anonymous contemporaries in an educated, middle-class citizenry. Specific queries, which directed attention instead to biographies and experience, sometimes elicited narrations of interaction with consociates which was memorable for the immediate awareness it engendered of a gap between practical abilities and interactional others' expectations.

In broadly similar ways, some Malays in Pontianak were able to evaluate their and others' fluency in Indonesian not with reference to social groups (like the town's Tio Ciu–speaking residents) but to locales (residents of Jakarta and Java). Some newcomers to Kupang, on the other contrary, could associate standard

Indonesian not with the city but the *daérah*, "back home," where they grew up speaking Indonesian in accord with the diglossic norm.

Similar ambiguities appeared in Chinese and Dayaks descriptions of themselves as competent in Pontianak's vernacular, but not as speaking it in any particular scenario. These too can be interpreted as stemming from different orientations to typifications and experiences of life in Pontianak. Their descriptions of competence, in the abstract, presupposed senses of alignment with urban contemporaries, Malay or otherwise. Responses to queries about their dealings with others, tied more closely to interactional scenarios, were based more on memories of engagements with urban consociates.

Despite the great interpretive space between a few remarks about talk, and issues of national belonging, this approach provides a broadened version of the value of the Indonesian paradox. It helps to situate that language between subjective, ambient senses of anonymous fellow citizens in the modern nation, and situated experiences of that modernity in one's engagements with others.

Lexicons of Modernity

Indonesians routinely flout the regime of the standard by making easy recourse to referentially useful English lexicons, resulting in conspicuously "mixed" use that has long been a target for critical commentary. It can be reviewed here by considering the relative values of Indonesian and English as national and global lingua francas.

Use of English terms in Indonesia is a recurring theme in what can be called, with James and Lesley Milroy (1985), the "complaint tradition" of standard Indonesian. Before the rise of the New Order the appearance of English in public discourse was diagnosed by some as a means for elites to assert their status in a modernizing nation, or a legacy of Javanese associations between language and power, or as symptomatic of a lack of confidence in Indonesian itself (Anderson 1966; Salim 1977; Errington 1986; Zentz 2017; Martin-Anatias 2018a, 2018b). In a neoliberalizing climate some now fear that an English-speaking elite may be abandoning Indonesian altogether (see, e.g., Akuntono 2011).[5] Others tie young persons' ways of incorporating English into their vernacular speech— Engdonesian, as Heryanto (2005) calls it—to a lack of interest in studying the standard language (Francisca 2008).

All such anxieties stem from the status of English as a foreign language (*bahasa asing*) and frame it as an issue of "national politics" (recalling a phrase quoted in Chapter 1). But varieties of English have become less "foreign" than global as they become less associated with native speaking citizens of Anglophone nations. As noted in Chapter 1, this process became evident in controversy in the 1990s over the category "native speaker of English." Now competences in English have become widely commodified in the simple but important sense (Block 2018) that varieties of the language are being acquired (bought) and taught (sold) in the absence of native speakers. This pedagogical shift reflects dynamics of globalization in which English has become more of a lingua franca, and so more like Indonesian.

Traditionally, English was taught as a foreign language (EFL) by a native English speaking teacher (NEST), a self-evidently privileged "owner" of English and citizen of what Kachru (1985) calls an "inner circle" nation: the United Kingdom or its former settlement colonies. Besides explaining and drilling, the NEST displays the full range of characteristics of maximally fluent speech, many too subtle to be described or, for many students, acquired. Under this paradigm students are presumed to be best served by "natural models" they may imitate, if never equal.

A newer pedagogy, designed to teach competences in English as a second language (ESL), developed mainly in what Kachru called "second circle" nations: former exploitation colonies of Anglophone powers. Under this paradigm nonnative English-speaking teachers (NNESTs) can help students who often have competences in local, markedly nonstandard varieties of English. The primary objects of pedagogy are literacy-linked varieties of English, understood at least tacitly to be in diglossic-like relations with "low," vernacular, or informal varieties.

Increasingly accepted now is the pedagogy of English as a lingua franca (ELF), often motivated with explicit critiques of "native speakerism" (see, e.g., Holliday 2006; Houghton and Hashimoto 2018). In Indonesia, as elsewhere, this pedagogy presupposes what Zein calls a "localised orientation" and "a shift from a monocentric approach, represented by the EFL and ESL perspectives, to a polycentric approach, represented by perspectives such as English as an international language (EIL) . . . and English as a lingua franca (ELF)" (2020: 46). Similar observations about the pedagogy of English in Indonesia have been made by Fan Fang (2017) and Kramadibrata (2016), who identifies a weakening of the "halo" effect that is now less supported by what he calls the "Native Speaker Fallacy."

Nonnative speakers may be more effective teachers of ELF because they have experiences and pedagogical goals centered not on native-like fluency but maximally portable intelligibility. They may be better able than native speakers of English to identify transfer effects from students' (ontogenetically) native languages that most impede their intelligibility in English. They may be more adept also at finding phrasings or manners of speaking ("workarounds") that are distinctly nonnative, but also intelligible in more contexts for native speakers of more languages (see, for instance Jenkins 2007; Bhatt 2017).

Strategies oriented not to sounding "more" like a native speaker of English, but "less" like a native speaker of some other language, are of interest here because they parallel pedagogical techniques proposed (but not implemented) for standard Indonesian. One such suggestion, made some time after the debates discussed in Chapter 1, came from the noted literary figure Ajip Rosidi. His preference, were it possible, would be for Chinese residents of Pontianak to be accepted everywhere as exemplars of standard Indonesian speech. But he recognized that to be an impossibility, and proposed instead that teachers be trained to help students identify and reduce those "interference" effects from their native languages that most strongly marked their spoken Indonesian. Implementing this "subtractive" approach would presuppose as a reference point the regime of the standard Indonesian as "agreed on by all parties" (Rosidi 2010: 95).[6]

Students taught in this way to sound "less ethnoregional" would acquire Indonesian with the same "touch of neutrality" attributed to global English (Ammon 2013: 117). This narrow point of pedagogy rests on what Widdowson called with regard to International English the "virtual presence" of standard Indonesian, which is "variously actualized ... by communities adapting it to their changing needs" (1997: 142).

In Chapter 1, I tied developmentalist metrics of referential utility and territoriality to the official privileging of unnative/anonymous Indonesian over native/ authentic ethnoregional languages. But these abstract, scalar metrics apply also to relations between Indonesian and unnative, global English. Insofar as the latter enables referential engagements with more topics, in more places, with wider ranges of interlocutors, this comparability can be a source of anxiety. It can surface in criticisms of "gratuitous" uses of English as a threat to Indonesian's "value" or "quality" (*mutu*; see, for instance, Ratna Hidayati 2007). Julia Suryakusuma, reflecting on difficulties in translating her English writings, concluded that Indonesian is a "poorly defined" language, and that its nation must be likewise "poorly defined indeed" (2013: 427).

This same comparability surfaces in ambivalent governmental policies and offices, where "the use of English as a foreign language seems to be discouraged ... as a means to preserve Bahasa (Indonesia), but on the other hand, some governmental institutions require English in their recruitment requirements" (Muhammad Beni Saputra 2018).[7] These testify to what can be called, borrowing a phrase from the Philippine protonationalist José Rizal (as translated by Anderson 1998), the specter of comparison that may accompany Indonesians' recourse to the language of global (not national) modernity.

In informal contexts, however, beyond the purview of the regime of the standard, differences of provenance of lexical material from two lingua francas can be less salient. Elements of both enable talk among members of an educated middle class which blurs lines between the national and global. Such patterns of everyday talk have parallels in literary genres that have emerged in post–New Order Indonesia. The literary critic Manneke Budiman describes novels by Dewi Lestari and Abidah El Khalieqy, for instance, as being located in a "multilingual world where rigid boundaries of nationality no longer apply" (2012: 60). He tacitly identifies Jakarta as that "busy intersection" where Indonesian "is losing its dominance as a 'national' language and becoming one of many 'international languages' . . . [with] a new place among the diverse and egalitarian forms of global identity that are emerging in the early 21st century" (2012: 47). But this observation can be "scaled down" and distanced from the cosmopolis to describe everyday talk in Middle Indonesian locales like Kupang and Pontianak.

From Last Wave to Next Wave?

A plurality of other-than-standard varieties of Indonesian may now covertly complement and enhance values of the Indonesian paradox in the nation at large. If so, another story of Indonesian's development is needed, on that looks beyond its role in a state-driven program aimed at "catching up" with nations of First World. Some of those ostensibly monoglot nations, located now in the Global North, are also being "buffeted in the current global dispensation," and their citizens may be "no longer so certain just what a normal language is" (Woolard 2016: 304). Three quick analogies might help to make the "miracle" of unnative Indonesian seem less of an outlier among the world's national languages.

One comparison can be made with uses of Catalan and Castillian (Spanish), another pair of structurally similar languages sharing many bivalent forms. This is possible thanks to Woolard's description of their uses among young persons who have come of age in the midst of nationalist struggle in Catalonia. The relation between Castillian and Catalan has become less clear, as is evident from debates about their values and uses among "spokesmen and activists" (as Hobsbawm would call them) on both sides of this debate.

Proponents of a Catalan nation privilege Catalan's distinctive authenticity, deep regional history, and literary tradition. Their unionist opponents cannot deny this claim, but instead identify Catalan as "provincial," and of less utility than Castillian. They argue that within and beyond the Spanish nation, cosmopolitan Castillian has more value for citizens of a modern nation, and in the Hispanophone world at large.

As these ideologies came to the fore in political debate, young persons in Catalonia (some of Hobsbawm's "ordinary citizens") acquired competence in both without internalizing a strong, normative sense of categorical difference between them. Woolard shows that they have acquired both languages "natively" but not as "naturally" distinct, and without a naturalistic sense that "a linguistic form exists independent of willful human intervention and that it naturally and directly corresponds to a social state of affairs" (2016: 7). She describes fine-grained ways that both languages figure in manners of speech that themselves serve "anti-essentialist, post-naturalist projects of linguistic identity" (Woolard 2016: 302). Structurally bivalent forms that figure in syncretic manners of speaking neutralize received distinctions between them as native languages of "us" or "them" (Woolard 1989).

"Natively bilingual" competences in Catalan and Castilian are being acquired, then, in the absence of a sense of what Woolard calls "sociolinguistic naturalness" that speakers of Indonesian have never had. This may be why her sketches of talk among young bilinguals in Catalonia resonate with those outlined here of talk oriented to "goal-oriented understanding[s] of personal and community authenticity as project rather than origin" (Woolard 2016: 302). Indonesian registers of urban modernity more broadly presuppose that "the future of Indonesia depends on individuals shaping themselves through self-cultivation and self-fashioning" (Smith-Hefner 2007: 190).

Comparisons between these political and cultural dynamics, one integrationist and one separatist, are possible because both involve languages that have become unmoored from self-evident, natural images of native speakership.[8] Less obvious, more diffuse comparisons can be drawn between Indonesian and languages of other Western European nations that are now undergoing de-standardization as documented by Studies of Standard Language Ideologies of Contemporary Europe (SLICE; see Kristiansen and Coupland 2011: 11). These provide empirical evidence of a "radical weakening or abandonment of the standard ideology" (Ghyselen et al. 2016: 77).

Appropriate examples here are younger Netherlanders who incorporate more visible and socially meaningful variation in their Dutch than do their elders. This variation is enabled by their weaker orientation to distinctly standard varieties, and a greater "reluctance to play by the rules of such standards" (Grondelaers, van Hout, and van Gent 2016: 142). New media have had collateral effects on what were formerly self-evident connections between talk and print-literate standards, resulting in a "downward relaxation of the standard leading to the emergence of regional and social varieties" (Grondelaers and van Hout 2011: 210). Young Netherlanders, like young Indonesians, seem increasingly accepting of multiple images (or typifications) of speakership "beyond the non-indexicality (neutrality) [i.e., anonymity] or mono-indexicality (superiority) of ideal standards" (Grondelaers, van Hout, and van Gent 2016: 131).[9]

I noted in Chapter 1 that the increased public visibility of other than standard Indonesians appears not to have eroded the public legitimacy of the regime of the standard. This situation may have analogs in Denmark, where changing pronunciations of Danish coexist with relatively stable perceptions of its distinct, standard forms. Kristiansen describes this as a process of demotization among persons who adhere to norms of standard Danish, but speak it in increasingly different, locally valued ways (Coupland and Kristiansen 2011: 28; see also Kristiansen 2016: 114).

A third comparison can be made between sociolinguistic dynamics described here and those ongoing in European urban centers. These have been identified as effects of expanding infrastructures of communication and mobility now identified with globalization. New flows or movements of persons and languages have given rise to conditions of social complexity there which Steven Vertovec first called "superdiverse" (2007). He proposed this term to properly distinguish the "diversity of diversities" as an unprecedented effect of global forces, confronting urbanites with the need to negotiate more and more various conditions of social difference.

Superdiversity has become a rubric for intersectional approaches to urban residents' locations, biographies, genders, gender relations, statuses, positions in multiple modes of stratification, and more. It helps connect conditions of locality with patterns of mobility, including motives for movement, patterns of movement, engagements with "home" nations at a distance, alignments or dissociations with other migrants, and so on.

Sociolinguists adopted the term "superdiversity" for their own work and, as Vertovec (2019: 128) himself pointed out in a review of the expanding literature on the topic, in calls for "methodological reassessment." (An influential charter for this movement is Blommaert and Rampton 2011.) Under this new rubric the complexities of linguistic encounters could be framed not as a residual topic, but as central for a "liberationist" approach to language. Those describing "superdiverse" conditions could see themselves as participating in a "transgressive moment" in the field's development, and as discarding "the false certainties of multiculturalism and established differences and hierarchies" (Arnaut 2012: 11).

Over this same period, "superdiversity" began to circulate as a "convenient euphemism" in "governing bodies concerned about the refugee crisis, the new migration, and the management of ethnolinguistic diversity" Aneta Pavlenko (2018: 161). A similar breaching or blurring of distinctions between academics (language study) and (language) politics was accomplished by Subahn Zein, who used "superdiversity" to document the need for reform to New Order era language policy. His concern was not with similarities between sociolinguistic dynamics in urban Europe and Indonesia, but the term's "liberating potential" (2020: 17) for foregrounding sociolinguistic complexities residualized by the regime of the standard. So too in Indonesian case, as Pavlenko notes more broadly, the term can shift attention "away from depressing treatment of linguistic diversity [like that discussed earlier] as an endangered phenomenon" (2018: 147).

Kupang and Pontianak could be seen, accordingly, as locales where are found very small parts of Indonesian's superdiversity. Different varieties of Indonesian were described relative to different dimensions of speakers ethnoregional backgrounds, native language competences, educational statuses, ages, social trajectories, patterns of mobility, and so on. Attention was given also to circuits of mobility that have made Kupang and Pontianak into larger, more complex scenes of urban encounter, where registers of Indonesian differ and overlap across contexts of encounter and communities of practice. My sketches of lexicons of modernity of English provenance could be seen as examples of what Blommaert and Backus (2012: 7) call truncated speech repertoires, and identify as characteristic of linguistic competences in superdiverse conditions.

But this comparison, like that with Catalonia, throws in relief broader differences between the social dynamics producing these conditions. Native Europeans can perceive (and fear) globalization's transnational, disintegrative effects as having the potential to transform (or destroy) their nations. Superdiversity in contemporary Middle Indonesia, or at least in towns like Kupang and Pontianak, has emerged from integrative dynamics over three generations, and appears to represent a point of transformation and continuity, recalling Cornelis Lay's observations, between eras of authoritarian and decentralized rule.

Describing Indonesian as "superdiverse" suggests a more ironic success story. What began as a project oriented to the kinds of modernity found in the West has had the unintended result of enabling a plurality of Indonesians. If the resulting conditions are superdiverse, then Indonesian has developed into an antecedent of conditions being driven elsewhere by dynamics of globalization. In this way it might "afford . . . privileged insight into the workings of the [globalizing] world at large" (Comaroff and Comaroff 2012a: 1).

From a different angle, with a focus on Indonesian's mobility, Zane Goebel has described the superdiversity of newly public registers of speech circulating through a range of mass media. He focuses on Indonesian as scripted for and spoken in television shows, so, representations of Indonesian speakership designed for public consumption. Diacritics of nonstandardness in these registers of speech include a few readily recognized linguistic forms drawn primarily from Sundanese, Javanese, and Jakarta's vernacular. Viewers can recognize the nonstandardness of such speech even if it differs from their own nonstandard ways of speaking.

In this way public figurings of private talk, that is, one-to-few relations of consociateship, become available for contemporaries to observe, not participate in, as members of a anonymous public. These displays of vernacular Indonesians invite recognition of similarities to their own manners of speaking, and so of a broader commonality between contemporaries who speak other Indonesians in other places. In this way mass media are acquainting Indonesian speakers with the "commonness or naturalness of linguistic superdiversity" in their nation at large (Goebel 2015: 170).

Mediated displays of consociateship can broaden Indonesians' acquaintance with the paradox of their national language, and anonymous others as sharers of the same but different language. These are images not of a formerly unified, unifying language now under threat, or undergoing fragmentation, but of an unnative language spoken in different but coexistent ways within the nation.

Linguistic superdiversity elsewhere in the world may be the harbinger of unprecedented change in urban locales and their nations; sociolinguistic dynamics in Kupang and Pontianak, I have argued, are mediating local versions of what Anderson called, in an earlier era, a "partly subconscious project for the assumption of modernity" (1966: 89). Though some are more marginal than others they incorporate, through Indonesian, the local and national alike.

Notes

1. A morpheme-by-morpheme translation that better reflects the simple juxtaposition in phrases would be "Diverse that, unitary that."
2. Other examples are provided by Zein (2020: 136) and Anthony Jukes (2015), who makes similar observations about the prestige of varieties of Malay spoken in the two largest towns of Sulawesi. Jukes describes the variety spoken in Makassar as "a relatively recent mixture of the local language Makassarese and standard Indonesian."
3. "Déngan alasan ingin menyesuaikan diri déngan lingkungan méréka menggunakan bahasa Melayu Pontianak dalam berinteraksi déngan penduduk asli. Namun, bahasa Melayu yang méréka gunakan bukan bahasa Melayu yang sebenarnya, melainkan bahasa Indonesian déngan dialèk Melayu."
4. A different discussion has developed about the "death" of polite varieties of Javanese, often called the speech levels. A solution to that problem, analogous to the challenge of national language development, has been proposed by Herudjati Purwoko (2011). A more comprehensive and situated description, centered on rural speakers in East Java, is van der Klok (2019). Wahyu Widodo (2017) shows how class distinctions discussed in Chapter 1 are reproduced in much writing, and how they pose an obstacle for efforts to "save" Javanese.
5. On related worries centered on the founding of International Standard Schools (Sekolah Bertaraf International), see Zentz (2017).
6. "[B]ahasa Indonésia yang disepakati oleh semua pihak."

7. Similar senses of ambivalence are expressed by college students who were interviewed by Lauren Zentz (2017) in Java. On use of the word meaning language (*bahasa*) in place of the name of Indonesian (*bahasa Indonesia*), see Lindsay (2006, 2013).

8. Similarly destabilized but less visible issues of speakership play into language-centered assertions of subnational autonomy, now thematic in literature on endangered languages. See, for instance, Jaffe (2015); McEwan-Fujita (2008); and O'Rourke & Walsh (2018). For accounts of other situations in which the category "native speaker" has become destabilized, see Pujolar and O'Rourke (2016); Doerr (2009); Escudero and Sharwood-Smith (2001); and Kramsch (2012).

9. This can be linked to what Heryanto (2014: 190) calls the "primarily orality-oriented" youth of Indonesia, now further engaged heavily with digital and mass media. On the recent visibility of vernacular "youth language" in Indonesian literature, see Dwi Noverini Djenar (2012). On the increased visibility of "mixed" Indonesian in a burgeoning mediascape, see also Zentz (2017). Analogous, mediatized decouplings of images of speakership and norms of print literacy, principally in Europe, are discussed in Androutsopoulos (2011).

Appendix 2.1. Selected Responses from Kupang Residents to the Queries:

Do you ever feel awkward speaking Indonesian? In what situation?

Apakah anda pernah merasa kaku waktu berbahasa Indonésia? Dalam situasi apa?

ZAN: 22, female, college student, Kupang native

Pernah, sangat pernah. Pada saat wawancara untuk melamar pekerjaan. Ketawa ketawa terus, malah béta yang langsung, apa? Kasih lelucon gitu, terus, dong tanya pakai bahasa Indonésia tapi béta nggak, jawab-jawab pakai bahasa Indonésia tapi di tengah-tengah sisip bahasa Kupang.

Yes, often, when I interview while applying for a job. I laugh, sometimes to, uh, tell a joke [tr. to loosen things up]. So if they ask questions in standard Indonesian but I don't—I answer using Indonesian but *bahasa Kupang* slips in.

DWI: 22, college student, Kupang native

Pernah. Di dalam kelas, sehari-hari *bahasa Kupang*. (Kalau déngan teman-teman?) Kaku juga.

Yes. In class, because everyday I use *bahasa Kupang*. (What about with friends?) Besides that, speaking to friends in Indonesian I feel awkward.

YNC: 25, female, college student, Kupang native

Pernah, di tempat-tempat yang resmi. Di—seperti di dalam kelas kalau mémpréséntasikan sesuatu, harus pakai bahasa Indonésia yang baik dan benar. (Terus? Kakunya di mana?) Karena sering pakai bahasa Kupang, maka rasa ganjil.

Yes, for instance in formal situations. Like in front of class when presenting something, we have to use good and true Indonesian. (So, how is it awkward?) Because we use *bahasa Kupang* so often it makes us feel awkward.

Appendix 3.1. Proportions of Indonesian *lagi* vs. Malay *gèq, giq* (more, again)

% Indonesian (min. 5 tokens)	≥ 0	≥ .1	≥ .2	≥ .3	≥ .4	≥ .5	≥ .6	≥ .7	≥ .8	≥ .9	1 (avg.)
Malay native Less educated (21)				2	1	8	1	6	2	1	0 (.6)
Malay native Educated (21)			1		2	1	3	2	5	1	6 (.74)
Malay newcomer (23)						6	1	2	6	3	5 (.76)
Dayak (18)						3	2	1	2	5	5 (.8)

Appendix 3.2. Proportions of Indonesian *juga* vs. Malay *gaq*

% Indonesian Minimum 10 tokens	≥ 0	≥ .1	≥ .2	≥ .3	≥ .4	≥ .5	≥ .6	≥ .7	≥ .8	≥ .9	1 (avg.)
Native Malay, Less educated (22)	20	1			1						(.02)
Native Malay, Educated (12)	5	1		2	1		1	1			(.2)
Newcomer Malay (17)	5		2	1	1		1		3		(.24)
Dayak (14)	1	1	3	2	1		1	1	3		(.38)

Appendix 3.3. Selected Responses from Pontianak Residents to the Queries:

Do you ever feel awkward speaking Indonesian? In what situation?

Apakah anda pernah merasa kaku waktu berbahasa Indonésia? Dalam situasi apa?

Note: Standard Indonesian forms are in roman typeface; Pontianak Malay forms are in italics with schwa transcribed.

JON: 22, male Dayak, college student

Pernah, sih, Ès Èm Pé. (Interviewer queries: Bisa bercerita?) Karena waktu itu kan, Ès Dé itu di kampung kan, jadi bicara dengan temen-temen yang Ès Dé itu masih ini apa, bahasa, bahasa kampong kan? Pas ketika SMP itu udah banyak sekali bahasa yang apa? Yang menyatu di situ. Ndak cuman bahasa dari kampong saya itu. Jadi pas waktu itu, yang bahasa saya itu, cuma saya sendiri gitu kan? Kan lainnya kebanyakan bahasa Melayu karena mémang di situ banyak Melayu kan? Jadi ini omong bahasa Indonésia agak, agak canggung gitu ya? Tapi udah kelas dua kelas tiga ndak, udah lancer.

Yes, when I was in middle school. (Can you talk about it?) Because in elementary school in my neighborhood, I would talk with my friends from school in the language of the neighborhood, right? So when I got to middle school there were a lot of languages which, uh, came together there. Not just the language of my neighborhood, so my language was just mine alone, right? The others were mostly speaking Malay, because there were a lot of Malays there. So speaking Indonesian was a little awkward, right? But by class two and three it wasn't; I had become fluent.

MAH: 23, male Dayak, college student

Pernah, sewaktu pertama kali datang ke Pontianak karena terpengaruh bahasa daérah. (Interview queries: Bisa ceritakan sedikit?) Seperti waktu saya katakan kemarin, yang kalau kita masalah bergaul gitu kan? Terus berbicara misalnya untuk bercerita sama orang lain kan? Gimana pada saat itu kita berbicara kan kita berbicara kan itu logat logat kita itu logat bahasa daérah kita akhirnya, orang kan terhéran kan, apa itu, bahasa gaya bahasanya, tertawa sendiri jadinya. Kita tertawa nah gitu kadang gitu.

The first time I came to Pontianak because of the influence of my regional language. (Can you talk about it?) Like what I told you the other day, when, if we have a problem being sociable right? Talking, for instance, and telling something to others? So at the moment we're talking, we're talking in dialect, our dialect, the language of our region. So finally the person is puzzled, "What language, what kind of language is that?" and he laughs to him/herself, so we laugh. Sometimes that's what happens.

MUK: 18, Malay college student from Pontianak

Pernah . . . waktu kita harus ngomong secara langsung déngan orang yang benerbener dari kota gitu dari Jakarta misalnya atau dari. . . . Soal Jakarta itu di *Jawə* itu kan? Bandung bener-bener pakai bahasa Indonesia yang baku jadi kaku kadang-kadang ceplosan kadang-kadang bahasa Melayu.

When we have to speak directly with people really from cities that are really, like from Jakarta for instance from . . . the thing is Jakarta is on Java, right? In Bandung [people] really use standard Indonesian, so it's awkward when I blurt out Malay.

GHO, 23, male Malay student from Sintang

Pernah, forum-forum resmi ataupun proses perkuliahan. . . . Waktu-waktu diskusi ataupun waktu ngasih matèri, pernah *kite* sangkutlah ya? Yang *pertame* mémang, kalau kité omong *bahasé* Indonesia *bahasany*é nyangkut dixxx karena itu memang dialèk atau logat. Tatap itu ndak ilanglah logat itu. Memang ya agak susahlah, logat agak susah kita ngilangkan. Sedikit banyaknya nyangkut. Nyangkut dari logatnya, kemudian, *adé* juga *bahasé-bahasé* yang *tadèkny*é yang bukan bahasa baku, terucapkan pada waktu kita pengin omong.

In official forums, or during lectures. When engaged in discussion or providing study materials, sometimes I (we) get caught [lit. hooked]. First thing, certainly if we speak Indonesian it carries over [a few syllables indistinct] because it's dialect, or accent. That doesn't disappear. It's really pretty difficult, the accent is hard to eliminate. More or less it carries over. Carries over in the accent, and (elements of) languages that aren't standard get accidentally spoken when we want to converse.

REFERENCES

Adelaar, A. 2004. Where does Malay come from? Twenty years of discussions about homeland, migrations and classifications. *Bijdragen tot de Taal-, Land- en Volkenkunde* 160 (1):1–30.

Agha, A. 2007. *Language and Social Relations*. Cambridge, UK: Cambridge University Press.

Akuntono, I. 2011. Para elite pun masih "menginggriskan" Bahasa Indonesia [The elite still "English" their Indonesian]. *Kompas*, October 30. http://edukasi.kompas. com/read/2011/10/30/16080625/Para.Elite.Pun.Masih.Menginggriskan.Bahasa. Indonesia. Accessed May 18, 2020

Alisjahbana, S. T. 1954. *Bahasa Indonesia dan Bahasa Daerah* [Indonesian and ethnic languages]. Djakarta: Pustaka Rakjat.

Alisjahbana, S. T. 1968. Fungsi standardisasi dalam pertumbuhan Bahasa Indonesia menjadi bahasa kebangsaan dan bahasa resmi modern [The function of standardization in the development of Indonesian into the national language and an official modern language]. In *Seminar Bahasa Indonesia* [Seminar on Indonesian], ed. Hari Kridalaksana and Djoko Kentjono, pp. 21–36. Jakarta: Nusa Indah.

Alisjahbana, S. T. 1976. *Language Planning for Modernization: The Case of Indonesian and Malaysian*. The Hague: Mouton.

Aman, I., and R. Mustaffa. 2009. Social variation of Malay language in Kuching, Sarawak, Malaysia: A study on accent, identity and integration. *GEMA Online Journal of Language Studies* 9 (1):63–76.

Amar Ola Keda. 2018. Salah satu bahasa daerah di NTT sekarat, penuturnya tinggal 2 orang [One of NTT's regional languages in its death throes with two remaining speakers]. *Liputan 6*, March 6. https://www.liputan6.com/regional/read/3384097/salah-satu-bahasa-daerah-di-ntt-sekarat-penuturnya-tinggal-2-orang. Accessed May 18, 2020

Ammon, U. 2013. World languages: Trends and futures. In *The Handbook of Language and Globalization*, ed. N. Coupland, pp. 101–122. Oxford: Wiley-Blackwell.

Anderson, B. 1966. The languages of Indonesian politics. *Indonesia* 1:89–116.

Anderson, B. 1991. *Imagined Communities: Reflections on the Origin and Spread of Nationalism*. New York: Verso.

Anderson, B. 1998. *Spectre of Comparisons: Nationalism, Southeast Asia and the World*. New York: Verso.

Androutsopoulos, J. 2011. Language change and digital media: A review of conceptions and evidence. In *Standard Languages and Language Standards in a Changing Europe*, ed. T. Kristiansen and N. Coupland, pp. 145–159. Oslo: Novus Press.

Appadurai, A. 1990. Disjuncture and difference in the global cultural economy. *Theory, Culture and Society* 1990:295–310.

Appadurai, A. 1995. The production of locality. In *Counterworks: Managing the Diversity of Knowledge*, ed. R. Fardon, pp. 208–209. New York: Routledge.

Arnaut, K. 2012. Super-diversity: Elements of an emerging perspective. *Diversities* 14 (2):1–16. UNESCO.

Arps, B. 2010. Terwujudnya Bahasa Using di Banyuwangi dan peranan media elektronik di dalamnya (Selayang pandang, 1970–2009) [The creation of the Using language in Banyuwangi, and the role of electronic media in that process (An overview, 1970–2009)]. In *Geliat bahasa selaras zaman* [Stretching language with the times: Change in languages in post-New Order Indonesia], ed. M. Moriyama and M. Budiman, pp. 225–246. Jakarta: Kepustakaan Populer Gramedia.

Aspinall, E., and G. Fealy. 2003. Introduction: Decentralization, democratization and the rise of the local. In *Local Power and Politics in Indonesia*, ed. E. Aspinall and G. Fealy, 1–11. Singapore: ISEAS.

Bamba, John, ed. 2008. *Mozaik Dayak: Keberagaman subsuku dan bahasa Dayak di Kalimantan Barat* [The Dayak mosaic: The variety of Dayak subgroups and languages in West Kalimantan]. Pontianak: Institut Dayakology.

Barker, J., E. Harms, and J. Lindquist. 2013. Introduction. In *Figures of Southeast Asian Modernity*, ed. J. Barker, E. Harms, and J. Lindquist, pp. 1–17. Honolulu: University of Hawaii Press.

Barnard, T., ed. 2004. *Contesting Malayness: Malay Identities across Boundaries*. Singapore: Singapore University Press.

Bhatt, R. 2017. World Englishes and language ideologies. In *The Oxford Handbook of World Englishes*, ed. M. Filppula, J. Klemola, and D. Sharma, pp. 84–102. Oxford: Oxford University Press.

Billig, M. 1995. *Banal Nationalism*. London/Thousand Oaks, CA: Sage.

Birnie-Smith, J. 2018. Chronotopically conditioned identities: the Chinese Indonesian context. Ph.D. dissertation Monash University.

Block, D. 2018. What on earth is 'language commodification'?. In B. Schmenk, S. Breidbach, and L. Küster, eds., *Sloganization in Language Education Discourse: Conceptual Thinking in the Age of Academic Marketization*. Bristol UK: Multilingual Matters. 121–141.

Blommaert, J., and A. Backus. 2012. Superdiverse repertoires and the individual. Tilburg Papers in Culture Studies, Paper 24. https://www.tilburguniversity.edu/ / research/institutes-and-research-groups/babylon/tpcs.

Blommaert, J., and B. Rampton. 2011. Language and superdiversity: A position paper. Working Papers in Urban Language and Literacies, Paper 70. https://newdiversit ies.mmg.mpg.de/fileadmin/user_upload/2011_13-02_art1.pdf.

Boellstorff, T. 2002. Ethnolocality. *Asia Pacific Journal of Anthropology* 3 (1):24–48.

Boellstorff, T. 2005. *The Gay Archipelago*. Princeton, NJ: Princeton University Press.

Bonfiglio, T. 2010. *Mother Tongues and Nations: The Invention of the Native Speaker*. New York: DeGruyter.

Bowden, J. 2012a. Local identity, local languages, regional Malay, and the endangerment of local languages in eastern Indonesia. Paper abstract, *The 16th International Symposium on Malay/Indonesian linguistics*. https://indoling.com/ismil/16/abstra cts.html. Accessed May 18, 2020.

Bowden. J. 2012b. Local languages, local Malay, and Bahasa Indonesia: A case study from North Maluku. *Wacana* 14 (2):313–332.

Bucholtz, M., and K. Hall. 2005. Identity and interaction: A sociocultural linguistic approach. *Discourse Studies* 7 (4–5):584–614.

Buchori, M. 1994. "Dialect" and "idiolect": Symptoms of the time. In *Sketches of Indonesian Society: A Look from Within*, pp. 21–31. Jakarta: The Jakarta Post and IKIP-Muhammadiyah Jakarta Press.

Budiman, M. 2012. Foreign languages and cosmopolitanism in contemporary Indonesian fiction: Redefining Indonesian identity after the New Order. In *Words in Motion: Language and Discourse in Post-New Order Indonesia*, ed. K. Foulcher, M. Moriyama, and M. Budiman, pp. 44–64. Singapore: National University of Singapore Press.

CAIREU Team. 2008. *Ethnic Dimension in Political Life: Study on Ethnic Preference in Pontianak Mayor Election*. Center for Acceleration of Inter-religious and ethnic understanding. Pontianak: Sekolah Tinggi Agama Islam Negeri.

Carruthers, A. 2017a. "Their accent would betray them": Undocumented immigrants and the sound of "illegality" in the Malaysian borderlands. *SOJOURN: Journal of Social Issues in Southeast Asia* 32 (2):221–259.

Carruthers, A. 2017b. Grading qualities and (un)settling equivalences: Undocumented migration, commensuration, and intrusive phonosonics in the Indonesia-Malaysia borderlands. *Journal of Linguistic Anthropology* 27 (2):124–150.

Chan, M. 2009. Chinese New Year in West Kalimantan: Ritual theatre and political circus. *Chinese Southern Diaspora Studies* 3:106–142.

Cole, D. 2010. Enregistering diversity: Adequation in Indonesian poetry performance. *Journal of Linguistic Anthropology* 20 (1):1–21.

Cole, D. 2014. Mobilizing voices and evaluations across representational boundaries—equitably and adequatively. *International Journal of the Sociology of Language* 227:175–192.

Collins, J. 1990. *Bibliografi Dialek Melayu di Pulau Borneo* [Bibliography of Malay dialects of the island of Borneo]. Kuala Lumpur: Dewan Bahasa dan Pustaka.

Collins, J. 1991. Rangkaian dialek Melayu di pulau Borneo [Malay dialects of the island of Borneo]. *Jurnal Dewan Bahasa* 35 (8):687–696.

Collins, J. 1998. *Malay, World Language: A Short History*. Kuala Lumpur: Dewan Bahasa dan Pustaka.

Collins, J. 2004. Contesting Straits-Malayness: The fact of Borneo. In *Contesting Malayness: Malay Identities across Boundaries*, ed. T. Barnard, pp. 168–180. Singapore: Singapore University Press.

Collins, J. 2006. *Borneo and the Homeland of the Malays: Four Essays*. Kuala Lumpur: Dewan Bahasa dan Pustaka.

Comaroff, J., and J. Comaroff. 2012a. *Theory from the South: Or, How Euro-America Is Evolving toward Africa*. London: Paradigm Publishers.

Comaroff, J., and J. Comaroff. 2012b. Theory from the South: Or, How Euro-America Is Evolving toward Africa. *Anthropological Forum* 22:113–131.

Conners, T. J., and J. Van der Klok. 2016. Language documentation of colloquial Javanese Varieties. In *Proceedings of the 2016 Annual Conference of the Canadian Linguistic Association*, ed.L. Hracs. https://cla-acl.artsci.utoronto.ca/wp-content/uploads/actes-2016/Conners_VanderKlok_CLA2016_proceedings.pdf. Accessed December 28, 2020.

Coupland, N., and T. Kristiansen. 2011. SLICE: Critical perspectives on language (de)standardization. In *Standard Languages and Language Standards in a Changing Europe*, ed. T. Kristiansen and N. Coupland, pp. 11–35. Oslo: Novus Press.

Davidson, J. 2007. Culture and rights in ethnic violence. In *The Revival of Tradition in Indonesian Politics: The Deployment of Adat from Colonialism to Indigenism*, ed. J. S. Davison and D. Henley, pp. 224–246. New York: Routledge.

Davidson, J. 2008. *From Rebellion to Riots: Collective Violence in Indonesian Borneo*. Madison: University of Wisconsin Press.

Djenar, Dwi Noverini. 2012. Almost unbridled: Indonesian youth language and its critics. *South East Asia Research* 20 (1):35–51.

Djenar, Dwi Noverini. 2015. Style and authorial identity in Indonesian teen literature: A "sociostylistic" approach. In *Language and Identity across Modes of Communication*, ed. Dwi Noverini Djenar, Ahmar Mahboob, and Ken Cruickshank, pp. 225–249. Boston: DeGruyter.

Djenar, Dwi Noverini. 2016. That's how it is there: Place, self and others in Indonesian narrative. *Narrative Inquiry* 26 (2):402–429.

Djenar, Dwi Noverini. 2020. Adolescent interaction, local languages and peripherality in teen fiction. In *Contact Talk: The Discursive Organization of Contact and Boundaries*, ed. Z. Goebel, D. Cole, and H. Mann, pp. 108–125. London: Routledge.

Djenar, Dwi Noverini, M. Ewing, and H. Manns. 2018. *Style and Intersubjectivity in Youth Interaction*. Boston: DeGruyter.

Doerr, N., ed. 2009. *Native Speaker Concept: Ethnographic Investigations of Native Speaker Effects*. New York: Mouton de Gruyter.

Dove, M. 2011. *The Banana Tree at the Gate: A History of Marginal Peoples and Global Markets in Borneo*. New Haven, CT; Yale University Press.

Eckert, P. 2012. Three waves of variation study: The emergence of meaning in the study of sociolinguistic variation. *Annual Review of Anthropology* 41:87–100.

Eckert, P., and S. McConnell-Ginet. 1992. Think practically and look locally: Language and gender as community-based practice. *Annual Review of Anthropology* 21:461–490.

Ediruslan Pe Amarinza. 2001. Sumbangan bahasa daerah terhadap Bahasa Indonesia: sebuah tinjauan [Contributions of regional languages to Indonesian: an overiew]. *Bahasa daerah dan otonomi daerah: Risalah konferensi bahasa daerah* [Regional languages and regional autonomy: Papers from a conference on regional languages], ed. D. Sugono and A. R. Zaidan, pp. 153–164. Jakarta: Pusat Bahasa, Departemen Pendidikan Nasional Jakarta.

Elson, R. E. 2008. *The Idea of Indonesia*. Cambridge, UK: Cambridge University Press.

Enfield, N.. and Tanya Stivers, eds. 2007. *Person Reference in Interaction: Linguistic, Cultural and Social Perspectives*. Cambridge, UK: Cambridge University Press.

Englebretson, R. 2003. *Searching for Structure: The Problem of Complementation in Colloquial Indonesian Conversation*. Amsterdam: John Benjamins.

Errington, J. 1985. On the nature of the sociolinguistic sign: Describing the Javanese speech levels. In *Semiotic Mediation in Psychosocial Perspective*, ed. E. Mertz and R. Parmentier, pp. 287–310. San Diego: Academic Press.

Errington, J. 1986. Continuity and discontinuity in Indonesian language development. *Journal of Asian Studies* 45 (2):329–353.

Errington, J. 1988. *Structure and style in Javanese: A semiotic view of linguistic etiquette.* Conduct and communications series. Philadelphia: University of Pennsylvania Press.

Errington, J. 1998a. Indonesian's development: On the state of a language of state. In *Language Ideologies*, ed. B. Schieffelin, K. Woolard, and P. Kroskrity, pp. 271–284. Oxford: Oxford University Press.

Errington, J. 1998b. *Shifting Languages: Interaction and Identity in Javanese Indonesia.* Cambridge, UK: Cambridge University Press.

Errington, J. 2008. *Linguistics in a Colonial World: A Story of Language and Meaning.* Oxford: Wiley Blackwell.

Escudero, P., and M. Sharwood-Smith. 2001. Reinventing the native speaker or "What you never wanted to know about the native speaker so never dared to ask." *EUROSLA Yearbook* 1:275–286.

Ethnologue: Languages of the World, 20th edition. 2017. https://www.ethnologue.com/language/ind. Accessed December 12, 2018.

Evi Novianti. 2011. Menilik nasib Bahasa Melayu Pontianak [Examining the future of Pontianak Malay]. In *International Seminar: Language Maintenance and Shift*, July 2, ed. T. Mckinnon et al., pp. 70–74. Semarang: Master's Program in Linguistics, Diponegoro University.

Ewing, M. 2005. Colloquial Indonesian. In *The Austronesian Languages of Asia and Madagascar*, ed. A. Adelaar and N. Himmelman, pp. 227–258. London: Routledge.

Fan Fang. 2017. English as a lingua franca: Implications for pedagogy and assessment. *TEFLIN Journal* 28 (1):57–70. Malang, Indonesia: English Department. http://journal.teflin.org/index.php/journal/article/view/418/279. Accessed December 13, 2019.

Ferguson, C. 1959. Diglossia. *Word* 15:325–340.

Fishman, J. 1967. Bilingualism with and without diglossia; diglossia with and without bilingualism. *Journal of Social Issues* 23 (2):29–38.

Fishman, J. 1978. The Indonesian language planning experience: What does it teach us? In *Spectrum: Essays Presented to Sutan Takdir Alisjahbana on His Seventieth Birthday*, ed. S. Udin, pp. 333–339. Jakarta: Dian Rakyat.

Fishman, J., C. Ferguson, and J. Das Gupta, eds. 1968. *Language Problems of Developing Nations*. New York: Wiley.

Floresa. 2017. *Gunakan bahasa Manggarai, 8 siswa SMPN 4 Pocoranaka-Matim dihukum jilat closet* [For speaking Manggarai, 8 students at Junior High School 4 Pocoranaka-Matim ordered to lick the bathroom]. September 29. https://www.flor esa.co/2017/09/29/gunakan-bahasa-8-siswa-SMPN-4-Pocoranaka-Matim-dihu kum-jilat-closet/. Accessed April 3, 2020.

Foong Ha Yap. 2011. Referential and non-referential uses of nominalization constructions in Malay. In *Nominalization in Asian Languages: Diachronic and Typological Perspectives*, ed. Foong Ha Yap and K. Grunow-Hå, pp. 627–658. Philadelphia: John Benjamins.

Fox, J. 1977. *Harvest of the Palm: Ecological Change in Eastern Indonesia*. Cambridge, MA: Harvard University Press.

Francisca, H. 2008. Rendah, minat mempelajari bahasa Indonesia [Interest in studying Indonesian is low]. Kompas.com. http://nasional.kompas.com/read/2008/05/18/18493818/rendah.minat.mempelajari.bahasa.indonesia. Accessed February 9, 2011.

Furnivall, J. S. 1944 [1939]. *Netherlands India: A Study of Plural Economy*. Cambridge, UK: Cambridge University Press; Macmillan.

Gal, S. 2018. Visions and revisions of minority languages: standardization and its dilemmas. In *Standardizing Minority Languages: Competing Ideologies of Authority and Authenticity in the Global Periphery*, ed. P. Lane, J. Costa, and H. DeKorne, pp. 222–242. New York: Routledge.

Gal, S., and J. Irvine. 2001. Language ideology and linguistic differentiation. In *Regimes of Language: Ideologies, Polities, and Identities*, ed. P. Kroskrity, pp. 35–83. Santa Fe, NM: School of American Research.

Gal, S., and J. Irvine. 2019. *Signs of Difference: Language and Ideology in Social Life*. Cambridge, UK: Cambridge University Press.

Gal, S., and K. Woolard. 2001. Constructing languages and publics: Authority and representation. In *Languages and Publics*, ed. S. Gal and K. Woolard, pp. 1–12. Manchester, UK: St. Jerome.

Gazzola, M. 2014. *Evaluation of Language Regimes: Theory and Application to Multilingual Patent Organisations*. Amsterdam: John Benjamins.

Gellner, E. 1983. *Nations and Nationalism*. Oxford: Blackwell.

Ghyselen, A.-S., Lybaert, C., and Delarue, S. 2016. Studying standard language dynamics in Europe: advances, issues & perspectives. *Taal en Tongval*. 68 (2): 75–91.

Gil, D. 2010. Riau Indonesian: What kind of a language is it? *Linguistik Indonesia: Jurnal limiah masyarakat linguistik Indonesia* 28 (2):113–140.

Goebel, Z. 2002. When do Indonesians speak Indonesian? Some evidence from inter-ethnic and foreigner-Indonesian interactions and its pedagogic implications. *Journal of Multilingual and Multicultural Development* 23 (6):479–489.

Goebel, Z. 2008. Enregistering, authorizing and denaturalizing identity in Indonesia. *Journal of Linguistic Anthropology* 18 (1):46–61.

Goebel, Z. 2009. Semiosis, interaction and ethnicity in urban Java. *Journal of Sociolingusitics* 13 (45):499–523.

Goebel, Z. 2010a. Identity and social conduct in a transient multilingual setting. *Language in Society* 39 (2):203–240.

Goebel, Z. 2010b. *Language, Migration and Identity: Neighborhood Talk in Indonesia*. Cambridge, UK: Cambridge University Press.

Goebel, Z. 2015. *Language and Superdiversity: Indonesians Knowledging at Home and Abroad*. Oxford: Oxford University Press.

Goebel, Z. 2017. Language diversity and language change in Indonesia. In *Routledge Handbook of Contemporary Indonesia*, ed. R. Hefner, pp. 378–389. New York: Routledge.

Goebel, Z. 2020. Modeling contact talk on television. In *Contact Talk: The Discursive Organization of Contact and Boundaries*, ed. Z. Goebel, D. Cole, and H. Manns, pp. 126–139. London: Routledge.

Goebel, Z., D. Cole, and H. Manns. 2020. Theorizing the semiotic complexity of contact talk: Contact registers and scalar shifters. In *Contact Talk: The Discursive Organization of Contact and Boundaries*, ed. Z. Goebel, D. Cole, and H. Manns, pp. 1–17. London: Routledge.

Goebel, Z., A. Jukes, and I. Morin. 2017. Linguistic enfranchisement. *Bijdragen tot de Taal-, Land- en Volkenkunde* 173:273–295.

Goffman, E. 1981. Footing. In *Forms of Talk*, pp. 124–157. Philadelphia: University of Pennsylvania Press.

Grangé, P. 2015. The Indonesian verbal suffix *-nya*. *Wacana* 16 (1):133–166.

Grijns, C. D. 1981. Jakartan speech and Takdir Alisjahbana's plea for the simple Indonesian word-form. In *Papers on Indonesian Languages and Literatures*, ed. K. Anwar and N. Philips, pp. 1–34. Paris: Association Archipel.

Grijns, C. D. 1996. Malay: Its history, role and spread. Compiled by K. A. Adelaar and D. J. Prentice, in *Atlas of languages of intercultural communication in the Pacific,*

Asia, and the Americas, ed. S. Wurm, P. Mühläusler, and D. Tryon, pp. 673–693. Berlin/New York: Mouton de Gruyter.

Grimes, B. 2005. How bad Indonesian becomes good Kupang Malay: Articulating regional autonomy in West Timor. Paper given at Anthropology Symposium, Universitas Indonesia, Jakarta, July 12–15.

Grimes, C., and J. Jacob. 2008. *Kupang Malay Online dictionary*. UBB-BMIT, Kupang.

Grondelaers, S., and R. van Hout. 2011. The standard language situation in the low countries: Top-down and bottom-up variations on a diaglossic theme. *Journal of Germanic Linguistics* 23 (3):199–243.

Grondelaers, S., R. van Hout, and P. van Gent. 2016. Destandardization is not destandardization: Revising standardness criteria in order to revisit standard language typologies in the Low Countries. *Taal en Tongval* 68 (2):119–149. https://www. researchgate.net/publication/314272652_Destandardization_is_not_destandard ization. Accessed December 7, 2017.

Hackert, S. 2012. *The Emergence of the English Native Speaker: A Chapter in Nineteenth-Century Linguistic Thought*, Vol. 4: *Language and Social Processes*, ed. R. Watts and D. Britain. Berlin: DeGruyter.

Hawkins, M. 2009. Violence and the construction of identity: Conflict between the Dayak and Madurese in Kalimantan, Indonesia. In *The Politics of the Periphery in Indonesia: Social and Geographical Perspectives*, ed. M. Sakai, G. Banks, and J. H. Walker, pp. 153–172. Singapore: National University of Singapore Press.

Herudjati Purwoko. 2011. If Javanese is endangered, how should we maintain it? In *International Seminar: Language Maintenance and Shift*, July 2, ed. T. Mckinnon et al., pp. 16–27. Semarang: Master's Program in Linguistics, Diponegoro University.

Heryanto, A. 1987. Kekuasaan, kebahasaan, dan perubahan sosial [Power, language, and social change]. *Kritis: Jurnal Universitas Kristen Satya Wacana Salatiga* 1 (3):4–53.

Heryanto, A. 1989. Berjangkitnya bahasa-bangsa di Indonesia [The spread of language and ethnicity in Indonesia]. *Prisma* 18 (1):3–16.

Heryanto, A. 1990. The making of language: Developmentalism in Indonesia. *Prisma* 50:40–53.

Heryanto, A. 2005. Engdonesian: Rubrik Asal Usul [Column: Beginnings]. *Kompas*, October 30. https://arielheryanto.wordpress.com/2016/03/04/engdonesian/ . Accessed November 8, 2018.

Heryanto, A. 2007. Then there were languages: *Bahasa Indonesia* was one among many. In *Disinventing and Reconstituting Languages*, ed. S. Makoni and A. Pennycook, pp. 42–61. Clevedon, UK: Multilingual Matters.

Heryanto, A. 2014. *Identity and Pleasure*. Singapore: National University of Singapore Press.

Herzfeld, M. 1997. *Cultural Intimacy: Social Poetics in the Nation-State*. New York: Routledge.

Hidayati, Ratna. 2007. Bahasa Indonesia alami penurunan mutu [Indonesian undergoes a fall in value]. Blog post. Mantagisme. http://mantagisme.blogspot.com/2007/09/bahasa-indonesia-alami-penurunan-mutu.html. Accessed May 8, 2014.

Hill, D. T., and K. Sen. 2005. *The Internet in Indonesia's New Democracy.* New York: Routledge.

Hill, J., and K. Hill. 1986. *Speaking Mexicano: Dynamics of a Syncretic Language in Central Mexico.* Tucson: University of Arizona Press.

Hobsbawm, E. J. 1990. *Nations and Nationalism since 1780: Programme, Myth, Reality.* Cambridge, UK: Cambridge University Press.

Hoffman, J. 1973. The Malay language as a force for unity in the Indonesian archipelago, 1815–1900. *Nusantara* 4:19–35.

Hoffman, J. 1979. A foreign investment. *Indonesia* 27:65–92.

Holliday, A. 2006. Native-speakerism. *ELT Journal* 60 (4):385–387. https://doi.org/ 10.1093/elt/ccl030.

Hoogevorst, T. G. 2011. Some introductory notes on the development and characteristics of Sabah Malay. *Wacana* 13 (1):50–77.

Horn, L. 2001. *A Natural History of Negation.* Stanford, CA: Center for the Study of Language and Information.

Houghton, S. and Hashimoto, K. eds. 2018. *Towards Post-Native-Speakerism.* Singapore: SpringerLink. https://link.springer.com/book/10.1007/978-981-10-7162-1 Accessed May 18, 2020.

Hui, Yew-Foong. 2011. *Strangers at Home: History and Subjectivity among the Chinese Communities of West Kalimantan, Indonesia.* Chinese Overseas, Vol. 5: Leiden: Brill.

I Gusti Ngurah Oka. 1974. Ragam Ujar BI dan PBI [Spoken Indonesian and the teaching of Indonesian]. In *Problematik Bahasa dan pengajaran Bahasa Indonesia* [The problematic of language and teaching Indonesian], pp. 117–132. Malang: Alma Mater, IKIP Malang.

IPAC (Institute for Policy Analysis of Conflict). 2018. The West Kalimantan election and the impact of the Anti-Ahok campaign. Report no. 43.

Irvine, J. 1990. Registering affect: Heteroglossia in the linguistic expression of emotion. In *Language and the Politics of Emotion*, ed. C. Lutz and L. Abu-Lughod, pp. 126–161. Cambridge, UK: Cambridge University Press.

Jacob, J. 2014. A sociolinguistic profile of Kupang Malay, a creole spoken in West Timor, Eastern Indonesia. https://www.academia.edu/6011590/A_sociolinguistic_profile_of_Kupang_Malay_a_creole_spoken_in_West_Timor_Eastern_In donesia. Accessed June 19, 2020.

Jacob, J., and B. Grimes. 2006. Developing a role for Kupang Malay: The contemporary politics of an eastern Indonesian creole. Paper presented at the Tenth International Conference on Austronesian Linguistics, January 17–20, 2006, Puerto Princesa City, Palawan, Philippines.

Jaffe, A. 2015. Defining the new speaker: Theoretical perspectives and learner trajectories. *International Journal of the Sociology of Language* 231:21–44.

Jenkins, J. 2007. *English as a Lingua Franca: Attitude and Identity.* Oxford: Oxford University Press.

Jespersen, O. 1942. *A Modern English Grammar on Historical Principles: Morphology.* Heidelberg: C. Winter.

Jukes, A. 2015. Asserting peripherality in Sulawesi: Local varieties and the rejection of Jakarta-based norms. Paper given at the Nineteenth International Symposium on Malay/Indonesian Linguistics. June 12–14, Jambi, Indonesia.

Jurriëns. E. 2009. *From Monologue to Dialogue: Radio and Reform in Indonesia.* Leiden: KITLV Press.

Kachru, B. 1985. Standards, codification and sociolinguistic realism: The English language in The outer circle. In *English in the World: Teaching and Learning the Language and Literatures*, ed. R. Quirk and H. G. Widdowson, pp. 11–30. Cambridge, UK: Cambridge University Press.

Kamal, Mustafa, et al. 1984. *Struktur bahasa Melayu Sambas* [The structure of Sambas Malay]. Jakarta: Pusat Pembinaan dan Pengembangan bahasa, Departemen Pendidikan dan Kebudayaan [Center for the Development of Language, Department of Education and Culture].

Kamal, Mustafa, et al. 1986. *Morfologi dan sintaksis Bahasa Melayu Pontianak* [Morphology and syntax of Pontianak Malay]. Jakarta: Pusat Pembinaan dan Pengembangan bahasa, Departemen Pendidikan dan Kebudayaan.

Kaplan, R., and R. Baldauf. 1997. *Language Planning: From Practice to Theory.* Clevedon, UK: Multilingual Matters.

Kartinnen, T. 2005. Upriver migration in linguistic communities in Sekadau (West Kalimantan). In *The Languages and Literatures of Western Borneo: 144 Years of Research*, ed. James T. Collins and Hermansyah, pp. 273–287. Bangi Institut Alam dan Temadun Melayu, Universiti Kebangsaan Melayu.

Keane, W. 2003. Public speaking: On Indonesian as the language of the nation. *Public Culture* 15 (3):503–530.

Kementerian Pendidikan Nasional. 2009. Undang-Undang Republik Indonesia Nomor 24 Tahun 2009 Tentang Bendera, Bahasa, Dan Lambang Negara, Serta Lagu Kebangsaan [Law of The Republic of Indonesia number 24, year 2009, regarding the flag, language, and symbol of the nation, together with the national anthem]. https://peraturan.bpk.go.id/Home/Details/38661/uu-no.24.tahun.2009. Accessed May 18, 2020.

Kisyani-Laksono. 2011. Pangeleluri basa lan dialek Jawa [Stimulating the Javanese language and dialects]. Paper given at the 5th Javanese language conference, November 27, Surabaya. https://ki-demang.com/kbj5/index.php/makalah-kunci/1129-06-pangleluri-basa-lan-dialek-jawa/. Accessed August 3, 2020.

Kozok, U. 2016. Indonesian native speakers—myth and reality. https://indonesian-nline.com/native-speaker. Accessed July 16, 2021.

Kramadibrata, A. 2016. The Halo surrounding native English speaker teachers in Indonesia. *Indonesian Journal of Applied Linguistics* 5 (2):282–295.

Kramsch, Claire. 2012. Authenticity and legitimacy in multilingual SLA. *Critical Multilingualism Studies* 1 (1):107–128.

Kristiansen, T. 2016. Contemporary standard language change: Weakening or strengthening? *Taal en tongval* 68 (2):93–117.

Kristiansen, T., and Coupland N., eds. 2011. *Standard Languages and Language Standards in a Changing Europe*. Oslo: Novus Press.

Kuipers, J. 1998. *Language, Identity, and Marginality in Indonesia: The Changing Nature of Ritual Speech on the Island of Sumba*. Cambridge, UK: Cambridge University Press.

Kurylowicz, J. 1964. *The Inflectional Categories of Indo-European*. Heidleberg: C. Winter.

Lay, C. 2014. Growing up in Kupang. In *In Search of Middle Indonesia*, ed. G. van Klinken and W. Berenschot, pp. 147–170. Leiden: Brill.

Lay, C. 2016. "Middle Indonesia": Harapan baru bagi Indonesia ["Middle Indonesia": New hope for Indonesia]. Notes for a lecture and discussion at the Research Center for Politics and Government (POLGOV), Department of Politics and Government, University of Gajah Mada, and the publisher Obor. Yogyakarta, February 24. https://www.academia.edu/33441721/_Middle_Indonesia_Hara pan_Baru_Bagi_Indonesia. Accessed February 28, 2020.

Leirissa, R. Z., et al. 1983. *Sejarah Sosial Kota Kupang Daerah Nusa Tenggara Timur, 1945–1980* [Social history of the city of Kupang, in the province of Nusa Tenggara Timur, 1945–1980]. Jakarta: Departemen Pendidikan dan Kebudayaan, Direktorat Sejarah dan Nilai Tradisional. [The inventorization and documentation project for national history, Department of Education and Culture, Directorate of History and Traditional Values.

Leyden, Dr. 1837. Sketch of Borneo. In *Notices of the Indian Archipelago and Adjacent Countries*, ed. J. H. Moor, pp. 93a–109a. Singapore: No recorded publisher.

Liddle, W. 1988. *Politics and Culture in Indonesia*. Ann Arbor: University of Michigan Press.

Liliweri, Alo. 1994. Prasangka sosial dan komunikasi antaretnik: Kajian tentang orang Kupang, Nusa Tenggara Timur [Social prejudice and interethnic communication: Research on residents of Kupang, Nusa Tenggara Timur]. *Prisma* 12:3–21.

Lindsay, J. 2006. The malaise of *bahasa Indonesia*. *The Jakarta Post*, February 15. p. 4.

Lindsay, J. 2013. *Bahasa* what? *Tempo*, March 3, pp. 52–53.

Liu, A. 2015. *Standardizing Diversity: The Political Economy of Language Regimes*. Philadelphia: University of Pennsylvania Press.

Long, N. 2013. *Being Malay in Indonesia: Histories, Hopes, and Citizenship in the Riau Archipelago*. Singapore: National University of Singapore Press.

Maier, H. M. J. 1993. From heteroglossia to polyglossia: the Creation of Malay and Dutch in the Indies. *Indonesia* 56:37–65.

Maier, H. M. J. 2004. *We Are Playing Relatives: A Survey of Malay Writing*. Verhandelingen van het KITLV, vol. 215. Leiden: KITLV Press.

Maier, H. M. J. 2011. Melayu and Malay—A story of appropriate behaviour. In *Melayu—The Politics, Poetics and Paradoxes of Malayness*, ed. Manznah Mohamad and Syek Muhd Khairudin Aljunied, pp. 300–329. Singapore: National University of Singapore Press.

Manns, H. 2014. Youth radio and colloquial Indonesian in urban Java. *Indonesia and the Malay World* 42 (122):43–61.

Manns, H. 2019. Gaul, conversation and youth genre(s) in Java. In *Special Genres in and around Indonesia*, ed. A. Jukes, A. Shiohara, and Yati. *NUSA* 66:3–18.

Manns, H., D. Cole, and Z. Goebel. 2020. Indonesia and Indonesian. In *Contact Talk: The Discursive Organization of Contact and Boundaries*, ed. Z. Goebel, H. Manns, and D. Cole, pp. 29–39. New York: Routledge.

Martin-Anatias, M. 2018a. *Bahasa gado-gado*: English in Indonesian popular texts. *World Englishes* 37 (2):340–355.

Martin-Anatias, M. 2018b. Language selection in the Indonesian novel: Bahasa gado-gado in expressions of love. *South East Asia Research* 26 (4):347–366.

Mauranen, A. 2018. Conceptualizing ELF. In *The Routledge Handbook of English as a Lingua Franca*, ed. J. Jenkins, W. Baker, and M. Dewey, pp. 7–24. New York: Routledge.

McEwan-Fujita, E. 2008. Working at "9 to 5" Gaelic: Speakers, context, and ideologies of an emerging minority languAge register. In *Linguistic Diversity: Endangered and Minority Languages and Language Varieties*, ed. K. King, pp. 81–93. Washington, DC: Georgetown University Press.

Milroy, J., and L. Milroy. 1985. *Authority in Language: Investigating Language Prescription and Standardization*. London: Routledge and Kegan Paul.

Minza, W. M. 2012. Young migrants and education-to-work transitions in Pontianak, West Kalimantan. *The Asia Pacific Journal of Anthropology* 13 (1):64–75.

Minza, W. M. 2014a. *Growing Up and Being Young in an Indonesian Provincial Town*. Amsterdam: Academisch Proefschrift, University of Amsterdam.

Minza, W. M. 2014b. Ethnicity and young people's work aspirations in Pontianak. In *In Search of Middle Indonesia: Middle Classes in Provincial Towns*, ed. G. van Klinken and W. Berenschot, pp. 111–131. Leiden: Brill. Verhandelingen van het KITLV, Vol. 292. Leiden: Brill.

Mohamad, G. 2008. Gado-Gado. In *Bahasa! Kumpulan tulisan di majalah Tempo* [Language! Collected writings from *Tempo* magazine], ed. B. Bujono and L. S. Chudori, pp. 3–6. Jakarta: Pusat Data dan Analisa TEMPO.

Moriyama, M., and M. Budiman, eds. 2010. *Geliat bahasa selaras zaman* [Stretching language with the times: Change in languages in post-New Order Indonesia]. Jakarta: Kepustakaan Populer Gramedia.

Muhidin, Salut. 2014. Migration patterns: People on the move. In *Regional Dynamics in a Decentralized Indonesia*, ed. H. Hill, pp. 317–341. Singapore: ISEAS Yusof Ishak Institute. https://muse.jhu.edu/book/35178. Accessed January 9, 2020.

Musgrave, S. 2014. Language shift and language maintenance in Indonesia. In *Language, Education, and Nation-building: Assimilation and Shift in Southeast Asia*, ed. P. Sercombe and R. Tupas, pp. 87–105. New York:Palgrave Macmillan.

Muslich, M. 2010. *Bahasa Indonesia pada era globalisasi: Kedudukan, fungsi, pembinaan, dan pengembangan* [Indonesian in the era of globalization: Its position, function, construction, and development]. Jakarta: Bumi Aksara.

Muyskens, P. 1998. We are all native speakers. But of which language? In *The Native Speaker: Multilingual Perspectives*, ed. R. Singh, pp. 193–204. Thousand Oaks, CA: Sage Publications.

Na'im, A, and H. Syaputra. 2010. Kewarganegaraan, suku bangsa, agama, dan bahasa sehari-hari penduduk Indonesia. Hasil Sensus Penduduk [Nationality, ethnicity, religion, and everyday language of Indonesia's residents. Results of the 2010 Census.] Jakarta: Badan Pusat Statistik. http//sp2010.bps.go.id. Accessed January 9, 2020.

Nababan, P. 1991. Language in education: The case of Indonesia. *International Review of Education* 37 (1):115–131.

Nakassis, C. 2013. Youth masculinity, "style" and the peer group in Tamil Nadu, India. *Contributions to Indian Sociology* 47:245–269. doi: 10.1177/0069966713482982.

Nino Histiraludin. 2012. Bahasa Indonesia "membunuh" bahasa daerah? [Is Indonesian "killing" regional languages?] *Kompasiana*, October 3. https://www.kompasiana.com/ninohistiraludin/551804c7a33311ad07b663d2/bahasa-indonesia-membunuh-bahasa-daerah. Accessed Feb. 23 2022.

Nyarwi. Ahmad 2008. Faktor etnis dalam Pilkada [Ethnic factors in regional elections]. Kajian Bulanan. Edisi 09-Januari 2008. PT Lingakaran Survei Indonesia. https://www.academia.edu/3150565/The_Politics_of_Ethnicity_and_Identities. Accessed December 7, 2017.

Oetomo, D. 1996. Bahasa Indonesia dan kelas menengah Indonesia [Indonesian and the Indonesian middle class] In *Bahasa dan kekuasaan: politik wacana di Panggung Orde Baru* [Language and power: Politics of discourse under the New Order], ed. Y. Latif and I. S. Ibrahim, pp. 195–212. Bandung: Mizan Pustaka. [Orig. in *Prisma* 1989 (1):17–29.]

O'Rourke, B. and J. Walsh, eds. 2018. New speakers across language contexts: mobility and motivations. *Journal of Multilingual and Multicultural Development* 39 (5).

Paauw, S. H. 2008. The Malay Contact Varieties of Eastern Indonesia: A Typological Comparison. Ph.D. dissertation, State University of New York, Buffalo.

Pavlenko, A. 2018. Superdiversity and why it isn't: Reflections on terminological innovation and academic branding. In *Sloganization in Language Education Discourse: Conceptual Thinking in the Age of Academic Marketization*, ed. B. Schmenk, S. Breidbah, and L. Küster, pp. 142–168. Bristol: Multilingual Matters.

Peluso, N., and E. Harwell. 2001. Territory, custom and the cultural politics of ethnic war in West Kalimantan, Indonesia. In *Violent Environnments*, ed. N. L. Peluso and M. Watts, pp. 83–116. Ithaca, NY/London: Cornell University Press.

Pennycook, A. 2002. Mother tongues, governmentality, and protectionism. *International Journal of the Sociology of Language* 154:11–28.

Pisani, E. 2014. *Indonesia Etc.: Exploring the Improbable Nation*. New York: Norton.

Pramoedya Ananta Toer. 1963a. Setengah abad setelah Abdullah Munsji. *Minggu Bintang Timur: Lentera-Lembaran kebudajaan Bintang Timur*, August 25.

Pramoedya Ananta Toer. 1963b. Basa Indonesia sebagai basa revolusi Indonesia (1). *Minggu Bintang Timur: Lentera-Lembaran kebudayaan Bintang Timur*, September 22.

Pujolar, J., and B. O'Rourke. 2016. Theorizing the speaker and speakerness: Lessons learned from research on new speakers. In *New Speakers, Non-native Speakers: Towards a Post-national Linguistics*, ed. J. Pujolar and B. O'Rourke. [Draft paper.] https://www.academia.edu/30325038/Theorizing_the_speaker_and_speakerness_lessons_learned_from_research_on_new_speakers. Accessed March 19, 2021.

Pusat Bahasa. 2007. *Laporan Adibahasa* [Report on Indonesian]. Jakarta. Unpublished paper.

Pusat Penelitian Sejarah dan Budaya Departemen Pendidikan dan Kebudayaan. 1981/1982. *Adat Istiadat Nusa Tenggara Timur* [Customs of Nusa Tenggara Timur]. Jakarta: Proyek Penelitian dan Pencatan Kebudayaan Daerah.

Rafael, A. 2019. Interferensi fonologis penutur Bahasa Melayu Kupang ke dalam Bahasa Indonesia di kota Kupang. [Phonological interference in Indonesian among speakers of Kupang Malay in Kupang.] *Jurnal Penelitian Humaniora* 20:47–58.

Rahmawati, Neni Puji Nur, and Salmon Batuallo. 2007. *Suku Dayak di Kabupaten Pontianak Provinsi Kalimantan Barat* [Dayaks in the Pontianak subdistrict of the province of West Kalimantan]. Pontianak: Direktorat Jenderal Nilai Budaya, Seni dan film Departemen Kebudayaan dan Pariwisata.

Rampton, B. 2011. From "multi-ethnic adolescent heteroglossia" to "contemporary urban vernaculars." *Language & Communication* 31 (4):276–294.

Ravindranath, M., and Cohn, A. 2014. Can a language with millions of speakers be endangered? *Journal of the Southeast Asian Linguistics Society* 7:64–75.

Ridhoino Kristo Sebastianus Melano. 2018. Dedy: Yang membunuh bahasa daerah bukan karena kebijakan pemerintah tapi kita sendiri [Dedy: "The killing of regional languages is not because of government decisions but we ourselves"]. *Tribun Pontianak*, April 4. Tribunnews.com/2018/04/13/dedy-yang-membunuh-bahasa-daerah-bukan-karena-kebijakan-pemerintah-tapi-kita-sendiri. Accessed May 18 2020.

Rosdiawan, Ridwan, et al. 2007. Merajut perdamaian di Kalimantan Barat [Creating/knitting peace in West Kalimantan]. In *Revitalisasi kearifan local: Studi resolusi konflik di Kalimantan Barat, Maluku, dan Poso* [Revitalizing local wisdom: Studies in conflict resolution in West Kalimantan, Maluku, and Poso], ed. Alpha Amirrachman, pp. 20–107. Jakarta: International Center for Islam and Pluralism.

Rosidi, A. 2010. Lafal baku bahasa Indonésia. [The standard pronunciation of Indonesian]. In *Bus bis bas—Berbagai masalah bahasa Indonésia*. [Bus bis bas—Various problems in Indonesian], pp. 94–97. Jakarta: Pustaka Jaya.

Salim, Z. 1977. The growth of the Indonesian language: The trend towards Indo-Saxonization. *The Indonesian Quarterly* 5(2):75–93.

Sapto Pradityo. 2015. Benarkah Bahasa Indonesia 'membunuh' bahasa daerah? [Is it true that Indonesia is "killing" regional languages?] *Detiknews*, November 27. https://news.detik.com/berita/d-3082186/benarkah-bahasa-indonesia-membu nuh-bahasa-daerah/1. Accessed May 18 2020.

Saputra, M. B. 2018. No, English is not a threat to Bahasa Indonesia. *The Diplomat*. https://thediplomat.com/2018/11/no-english-is-not-a-threat-to-bahasa-indone sia. Accessed July 16, 2021.

Schuchardt, H. 1979 [1909]. On lingua franca. In *The Ethnography of Variation: Selected Writings on Pidgins and Creoles*, ed. and trans. T. L. Markey, pp. 26–47. Ann Arbor, MI: Karoma.

Schutz, A. 1978. *Phenomenology of the Social World*. Trans. G. Walsh and F. Lehnert. Evanston, IL: Northwestern University Press.

Seidler, S. 2009. Encounters with the mother tongue. In *Being There—The Fieldwork Encounter and the Making of Truth*, ed. J. Bornemann and A. Hammoudi, pp. 183–200. Berkeley: University of California Press.

Shiohara, Asako. 2010. Penutur bahasa minoritas di Indonesia bagian timur: Mempertanyakan keuniversalan konsep multibahasa. [Speakers of minority languages in Eastern Indonesia: Interrogating the concept of multilingualism] In *Geliat bahasa selaras zaman* [Stretching language with the times: Change in languages in post-New Order Indonesia], ed. M. Moriyama and M. Budiman, pp. 168–206. Jakarta: Kepustakaan populer Gramedia.

Shiohara, Asako. 2012. How universal is the concept of multilingualism? Minority language speakers in Eastern Indonesian. In *Words in Motion: Language and Discourse in Post-New Order Indonesia*, ed. K. Foulcher, M. Moriyama, and Manneke Budiman, pp. 101–126. Singapore: National University of Singapore Press.

Siegel, J. 1993. Dialect contact and koinéization: A review of *Dialects in Contact*, by Peter Trudgill. *International Journal of the Sociology of Language* 99:105–121.

Silverstein, M. 1996. Monoglot "standard" in America: Standardization and metaphors of linguistic hegemony. In *The Matrix of Language: Contemporary Linguistic Anthropology*, ed. D. L. Brenneis and R. K. S. Macaulay, pp. 284–306. Boulder, CO: Westview Press.

Simpson, B. 2009. Indonesia's "Accelerated Modernization" and the global discourse of development, 1960–1975. *Diplomatic History* 33 (3):467–486.

Singh, R., ed. 1998. *The Native Speaker: Multilingual Perspectives*. Thousand Oaks, CA: Sage Publications.

Smith-Hefner, N. 2007. Youth language, *gaul* sociability, and the new Indonesian middle class. *Journal of Linguistic Anthropology* 17(2):184–203.

Sneddon, J. 2002. Variation in informal Jakartan Indonesian: A quantitative study. *Linguistik Indonesia* 20 (2):127–157.

Sneddon, J. 2003a. *The Indonesian Language: Its History and Role in Modern Society*. Sydney: University of New South Wales Press.

Sneddon, J. 2003b. Diglossia in Indonesian. *Bijdragen tot de Taal-, Land- en Volkenkunde* 159 (4):519–549. doi:10.1163/22134379-90003741.

Sneddon, J. 2006. *Colloquial Jakartan Indonesian.* Canberra: Research School of Pacific and Asian Studies, Australia National University.

Steinhauer, H. 1994. The Indonesian language situation and linguistics: Prospects and possibilities. *Bijdragen tot de Taal-, Land- en Volkenkunde* 150 (4):755–784.

Subianto, Benny. 2009. Ethnic politics and the rise of the Dayak bureaucrats in local election. In *Deepening Democracy in Indonesia? Direct Elections for Local Leaders (Pilkada)*, ed. Maribeth Erb and Priyambudi Sulistiyanto, pp. 327–351. Singapore: ISEAS.

Sudagung, Hendro Suroyo. 2001. *Mengurai pertikaian etnis: Migrasi swakarsa etnis Madura ke Kalimantan Barat* [Studying ethnic conflict: Spontaneous Madurese migration to West Kalimantan]. Jakarta: Institut Studi Arus Informasi.

Suryakusuma, Julia. 2013. View point: Mind your (Indonesian) language! In *Julia's Jihad: Tales of the Politically, Sexually and Religiously Incorrect: Living in the Chaos of the Biggest Muslim Democracy*, pp. 427–430. Depok: Indonesia Komunitas Bambu.

Susilo Firman, et al. 1998. *Fonologi bahasa Melayu Sambas* [Phonology of Sambasa Malay]. Jakarta: Pusat Pembinaan dan Pengembangan bahasa, Departemen Pendidikan dan Kebudayaan.

Taeldeman, J. 2005. The influence of urban centres on the spatial diffusion of dialect phenomena. In *Dialect Change: Convergence and Divergence in European Languages*, ed. P. Auer, F. Hinskens, and P. Kerswill, pp. 263–283. Cambridge, UK: Cambridge University Press.

Tamtamo, K. 2018a. The compartmentalization of languages and identities among nationalist youth in Semarang. *Wacana* 19 (1):168–190.

Tamtamo, K. 2018b. Institution and market: Orders of multiple languages in Indonesian vocational education. *Multilingua* 37(5):429–454.

Tanasaldy, Taufiq. 2007. Ethnic identity politics in West Kalimantan. In *Renegotiating Boundaries: Local Politics in Post-Suharto Indonesia*, ed. H. S. Nordholt and G. van Klinken, pp. 349–372. Leiden: KITLV Press.

Tanasaldy, Taufiq. 2012. *Regime Change and Ethnic Politics in Indonesia: Dayak Politics of West Kalimantan*. Verhandelingen van het KITLV Leiden No. 278.

Tidey, S. 2010. Problematizing "ethnicity" in informal preferencing in civil service: Cases from Kupang, Eastern Indonesia. *Journal of Asia Pacific Studies* 1 (3):545–569.

Tidey, Sylvia. 2012. Performing the State: Everyday Practices, Corruption and Reciprocity in Middle Indonesian Civil Service. Ph.D. dissertation, University of Amsterdam.

Tidey, S. 2014. A divided provincial town: The development from ethnic to class-based segmentation in Kupang, West Timor. In *In Search of Middle Indonesia: Middle Classes in Provincial Towns*, ed. G. van Klinken and W. Berenschot, pp. 89–110. Leiden: Brill.

Tribun Wow. 2017. *Kronologi 8 siswa SMPN 4 Poco Ranaka dihukum jilat kloset! Begini penyelesaian masalahnya!* [Chronology of 8 students at junior high school Poco Ranaka who were forced to lick the bathroom! Here's how the matter was closed!]. https://wow.tribunnews.com/2017/09/30/kronologi-8-siswa-smpn-4-poco-ran aka-dihukum-jilat-kloset-begini-penyelesaian-masalahnya?fb_comment_id= 1495840263832682_1497221823694526 Accessed April 3, 2020.

Tule, P. 2000. Religious conflicts and a culture of tolerance: Paving the way for reconciliation in Indonesia. *Antropologi Indonesia* 63:92–108.

Valentijn, F. 1724–1726. *Oud en nieuw Oost-Indien, vervattende een naaukeurige en uitvoerige verhandelinge van Nederlands mogentheyd in die gewesten, benevens eene wydlustige behschryvinge der Moluccos, Amboina, Banda, Timor, en Solor, Jawa en alle de eylanded onder dezelve landbestieringen behoorend*ed. 5 vols. Dordrecht: Joannes van Braamand Amsterdam: Gerard onder de Linden.

Van der Klok, J. 2019. The Javanese language at risk: perspectives from an East Java village. *Language Documentation and Conservation* 13:300–345.

Van der Putten, J. 2010. Bongkar bahasa: Meninjau kembali konsep yang beraneka makna dan beragam fungsi [Opening up "language": Reconsidering a concept with various meanings and multiple functions]. In *Geliat bahasa selaras zaman: Perubahan bahasa-bahasa di Indonesia pasca-Orde Baru* [Stretching the language to fit the times: Changes in languages in post-New Order Indonesia], ed. M. Moriyama and M. Budiman, pp. 1–29. Jakarta: Kepustakaan populer Gramedia.

Van der Putten, J. 2012. Going against the tide: The politics of language standardization in Indonesia. In *Words in Motion: Language and Discourse in Post-New Order Indonesia*, ed. K. Foulcher, M. Moriyama, and M. Budiman, pp. 257–279. Singapore: National University of Singapore Press.

Van Klinken, G. 2007. Return of the sultans: The communitarian turn in local politics. In *The Revival of Tradition in Indonesian Politics: The Deployment of Adat from Colonialism to Indigenism*, ed. J. S. Davidson and D. Henley, pp. 149–169. New York: Routledge.

Van Klinken, G. 2014a. Introduction: Democracy, markets and the assertive middle. In *In Search of Middle Indonesia: Middle Classes in Provincial Towns*, ed. G. Van Klinken and W. Berenschot, pp. 1–32. Verhandelingen van het KITLV, vol. 292. Leiden: Brill.

Van Klinken, G. 2014b. *The Making of Middle Indonesia: Middle Classes in Kupang Town, 1930s–1980s*. Leiden: Brill.

Van Klinken, G., and W. Berenschot, eds. 2014. *In Search of Middle Indonesia: Middle Classes in Provincial Towns*. Verhandelingen van het KITLV, vol. 292. Leiden: Brill.

Vel, J. 2008. *Uma Politics: An Ethnography of Democratization in West Sumba, Indonesia, 1986–2006*. Leiden: KITLV Press.

Vertovec, S. 2007. Super-diversity and its implications. *Ethnic and Racial Studies* 30 (6):1024–1054.

Vertovec, S. 2019. Talking around super-diversity. *Ethnic and Racial Studies* 42 (1):125–139.

Wahyu Widodo. 2017. Hal yang rupang dan timpang dalam kebijakan perencanaan Bahasa Jawa. [Gaps and flaws in language planning for Javanese.] *Linguistik Indonesia* 35 (1):33–52.

Warner, M. 2002. Publics and counterpublics. *Public Culture* 14 (1):49–90.

Widdowson, H. 1997. EIL, ESL, EFL: Global issues and local interests. *World Englishes* 16 (1):135–146.

Wilson, A. 2004. *Intimate Economies of Bangkok: Tomboys, Tycoons, and Avon Ladies in the Global City*. Berkeley: University of California Press.

Wong Kon Ling, Jane. 2000. *The Sabah Malay Dialect: Phonological Structures and Social Functions*. Kota Kinabalu: Pusat Penataran Ilmu dan Bahasa Universiti Malaysia Sabah [Center for the promotion of knowledge and language learning], Universiti Malaysia Sabah.

Woolard, K. 1989. *Double Talk: Bilingualism and the Politics of Ethnicity in Catalonia*. Stanford, CA: Stanford University Press.

Woolard, K. 1999. Simultaneity and bivalency as strategies in bilingualism. *Journal of Linguistic Anthropology* 8 (1):3–29.

Woolard, K. 2016. *Singular and Plural: Ideologies of Linguistic Authority in 21st Century Catalonia*. Oxford: Oxford University Press. doi: 10.1093/acprof:oso/9780190258610.001.0001.

Wouk, F. 1991. Dialect contact and koinéization in Jakarta, Indonesia. *Language Sciences* 21:61–86.

Wright, S. 2003. *Language Policy and Language Planning: From Nationalism to Globalization*. Basingstoke, UK: Palgrave Macmillan.

Yuan, Bingling. 2000. *Chinese Democracies: A Study of Kongsis of West Borneo (1776–1884)*. Leiden: Research School of Asian, African, and Amerindian Studies, Universiteit Leiden.

Zein, S. 2020. *Language Policy in Superdiverse Indonesia*. Abingdon, UK: Taylor and Francis.

Zentz, L. 2015. The more things change the more they stay the same? Exploring a century of Indonesian language planning discourses. Tilburg Papers in Culture Studies, no. 133. Tilburg University. https://www.academia.edu/19342522/TPCS_133_The_more_things_change_the_more_they_stay_the_same_Exploring_a_century_of_Indonesian_language_planning_discourses_by_Lauren_Zentz.

Zentz, L. 2017. *Statehood, Scale and Hierarchy: History, Language and Identity in Indonesia*. Bristol, UK: Multilingual Matters.

Zhang, J., and Yanti, R. 2019. Notions of community and *intisari*: Reflections on researching language ideologies in multilingual eastern Indonesia. *Critical Mutilingualism Studies* 7(1). https://cms.arizona.edu/index.php/multilingual/article/view/175.

INDEX

accent
in Indonesian, 17
in Kupang Malay, 27–28, 30, 32, 33
in Pontianak Malay, 52–55, 57–58, 60,
65, 71, 72, 97–98
Adelaar, A., 21
adequation, 54, 62, 72
Agha, A., 12, 59, 84
Akuntono, I., 86
Alisjahbana, T., 5, 6
Alor, 42
Aman, I., 73, 74
Amar Ola Keda, 79
Ambon, 79
Ammon, U., 88
Anderson, B., 7, 14, 18, 82, 84–86, 88, 93
Androutsopoulos, J., 94
anonymity
of contemporaries, 82–86
ideology of, 6
of Indonesian, 6–7, 17, 72, 79, 88
of public citizenry, 19, 92
See also unnativeness
Anton Moeliono, 8, 9, 12, 78
Appadurai, A., 2, 84
Arabic, 13, 16
Arnaut, K., 91
Arps. B., 7, 20
Aspinall, E., 2
authenticity
of Catalan, 89, 90

of ethnoregional/"low" languages, 7
and expressiveness, 28
ideology of, 7
of speech, 79
of standard English, 16

Backus, A., 92
bahasa Betawi, 8, 14, 21. *See also bahasa
Jakarta*
bahasa daérah, 4, 8, 11, 86. *See also*
ethnoregional languages
bahasa gado-gado, 3, 81
bahasa gaul, 10, 46
bahasa Indonésia. See Indonesian
bahasa Jakarta, 8, 13, 21, 28, 57, 75
bahasa Kupang, 13, 23–25, 27, 40–41,
45–47, 57, 72, 95. *See also* Kupang
Malay
bahasa Melayu, 13, 68, 93, 96, 97. *See also*
Malay
bahasa Melayu Pontianak, 13, 49, 70, 80,
93. *See also* Pontianak Malay
bahasa Pontianak, 49, 57, 60, 63, 68, 72
Balukh, J., 26–28
Bamba, J., 50
Barker, J., 11
Barnard, T., 21
Batuallo, S., 73
Bhatt, R., 87
biaccentualism, 15, 31, 54–57, 61–66, 84
bilingualism, 7, 15, 18, 81, 90